A Nation *of* Associations

The Origin, Development and Theory of the Political Action Committee

by Alfred Balitzer

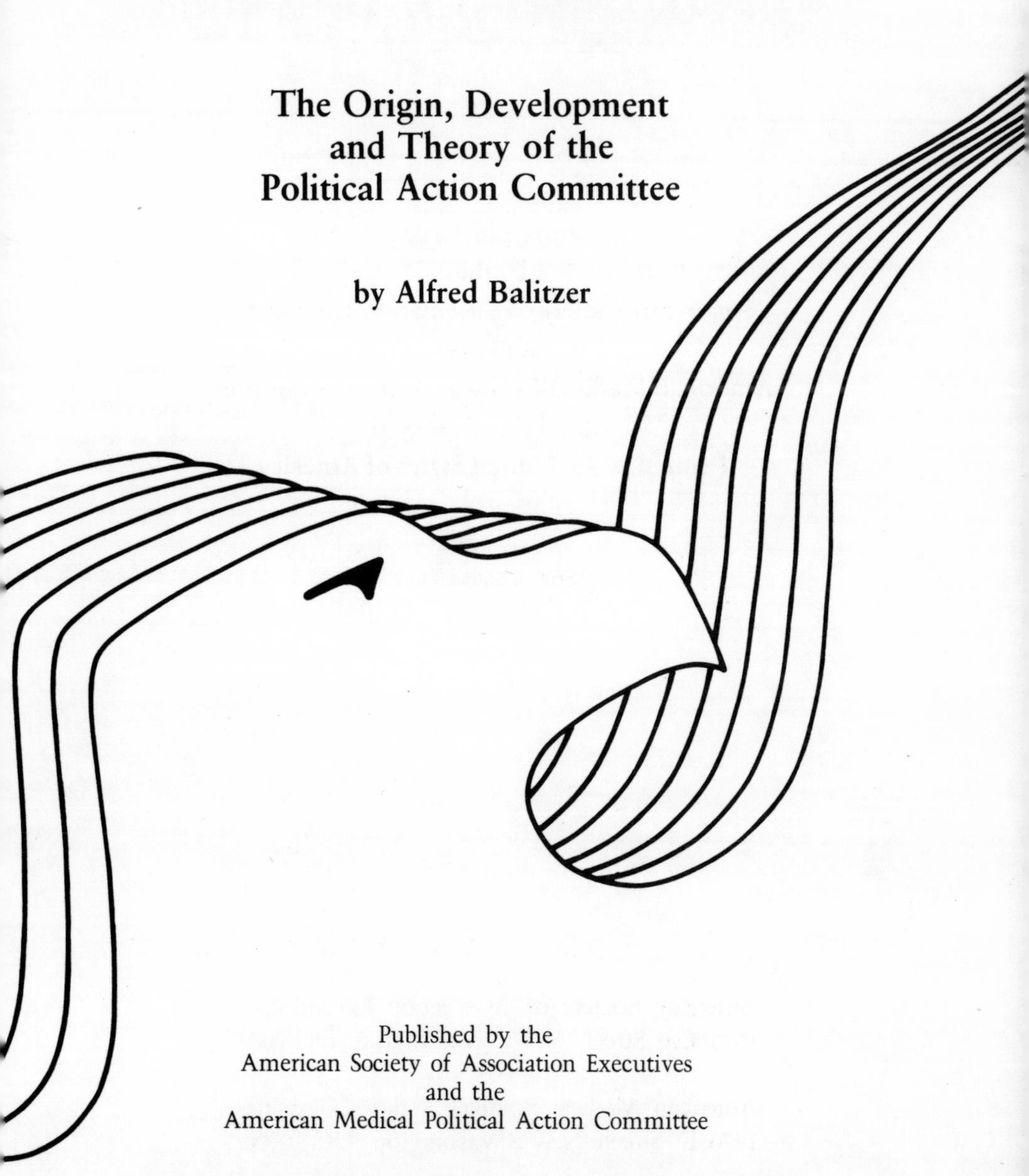

Published by the
American Society of Association Executives
and the
American Medical Political Action Committee

ISBN 0-88034-000-2

American Society of Association Executives
1575 Eye Street, N.W., Washington, DC 20005

American Medical Political Action Committee
1776 K Street, N.W., Washington, DC 20006

Contents

About the Author

Alfred Balitzer is an assistant professor of political science at Claremont Men's College and Claremont Graduate School. Among his publications are several pieces on American religion, including "Some Thoughts About Civil Religion," the "Political Implications of the Ecumenical Movement," and the "Civil Religion Debate." In addition, Dr. Balitzer has prepared studies on "The Commission Experience: Studies of Non-legislative Approaches to Redistricting," and "The Initiative and Referendum: A Study and Evaluation of Direct Legislation." For several years Dr. Balitzer has served as Executive Director of the California Congressional Recognition Project, and published in 1976, 1978 and in 1980 evaluations of the California Congressional Delegation entitled *Californians in Congress*. Dr. Balitzer also serves as the Director of Research for the Rose Institute of State and Local Government.

Born and reared in Los Angeles, California, Dr. Balitzer received his Masters degree from the University of Chicago and his Doctorate from Claremont Graduate School. He has taught at Claremont since 1971.

Preface

"In Praise of PACs" by Rep. Newt Gingrich (R-GA)

We are in a revolution in American politics. That revolution is being greatly undercovered by the press because the press is focusing on the wrong things.

With the campaign "reform" laws of the mid-seventies came profound changes in American politics. Wealthy people have been restricted in their direct contributions. There has been an explosive emergence of a whole new zone of activity, symbolized by the prevalence of political action committees. These PACs have brought a whole new generation of people into the world of campaign contributions, and they're tying political behavior in campaigns to political behavior in governing more tightly than has been the case in the last thirty years.

Political action committees are bringing informed interest groups out in the open, so that we can begin to see a real relationship among the way people behave in elections, the way people behave in contributions, and the way congressmen vote. PACs can move us away from what the Founding Fathers feared our democracy would drift toward: an *atomistic* society.

In the atomistic model of a free society, there is a general, vague "common good" which is normally given to us by a Ralph Nader or a John Gardner. It is communicated through television and then we, as 225 million individual atoms working in a plebiscitary system, say, "Yes. Do this. No, don't do that." That is precisely the Aristotelian vision of mob politics, which the Founding Fathers thought might be the end of this society.

The only workable alternative to that system is a *mediating institution* society, in which a great number of small sub-groups, acting separately, protect both the individual and the government. Mediating institutions prevent the government from crushing any individual and prevent individuals as groups from forming into a plebiscite which crushes the government and turns it into a tyranny.

Traditionally, we've had mediating institutions such as county courthouses and big-city machines. They are in decay. But a new mediating institution is emerging: the political action committee. It is not geographic but instead based on common interest. It's tied together by newsletters, mailgrams, and annual conventions. It's at least as accountable as was the big-city machine. After all, people don't *have* to contribute.

In order to attract contributions, the PAC has to in some way reflect the interests of the people who give to it. Because the PAC is organized, it allows the individual voter to know that somebody is watching out for his interest—and is probably doing a better job of it than is his congressman. That congressman, after all, has to represent 10,000 differing interests—or as many as will be found among his 500,000 constituents.

So the PAC is our new watchdog, legitimately looking out for the interests of its contributors. This pattern is as old as American politics. It's why Jefferson's farmers were opposed to Hamilton's shipowners and merchants. People who were elected by Jefferson's farmers tended to vote against the interests of Hamilton's shipowners and merchants. The idea behind PACs is nothing new. We are merely talking about a different structure, reflecting old patterns, that more openly relates campaign contributions to politicians' behavior in office.

People who say that PACs are bad are, in effect, saying that voters ought to elect people on one set of campaign promises who should then be allowed to do anything they want to in between campaigns. That's the bottom line: The campaign promises, and the contributions they encourage, should have no relationship to the actions of the people that the money and the promises elevate to Congress.

But that is rampant nonsense. To say that "special interests govern the Congress" assumes special interests are a monolith. I know from experience that they're not. For example, I found myself siding with Georgia Power and the rural electric co-ops by voting for coal slurry pipeline legislation—which was a vote against the railroads. A few weeks later I opposed the Eckhardt amendment to the rail deregulation bill, which was a vote for the railroads and against the interests of Georgia Power and the rural electric co-ops.

Which PAC is now supposed to own me as a congressman? Am I under the sway of the PACs who backed the pipeline or the PACs who favor the railroads? In each vote, I was on the side I thought correct for America's technological expansion. That was the only constant, and to talk of all-pervasive "special interests" is to assume constancy where there is little: the PACs will line up differently on different issues.

If Common Cause really wanted more people involved in politics, that organization would favor increasing the number of PACs as rapidly as possible—whether the new PACs reflected quality-of-life interest groups like the Sierra Club, age-based interest groups like the senior citizens associations, geographic interest groups like the neighborhood and regional organizations, or newly-emerging economic interest groups.

Once you get to 30,000 PACs, any congressman or candidate who is reasonably intelligent and articulate can knit together a coalition which will then have a contractual relationship with that congressman or candidate. The coalition will say: "We support you, we help you stay in politics, we expect you to represent us. If you're not going to represent us, tell us that and we'll find somebody else to support."

In the long run, the best defense against political action committees is more political action committees. The more of them there are, the harder it will be for any one, five, or ten to have any exaggerated impact. Al Smith said, "The only cure for the dangers of political action committees is more political action committees."

And to those who fear money in politics, let me say that we need more, not less, money in politics. PACs are not disgracing American politics. The disgrace, to cite a specific case, comes when Jay Rockefeller spends $31 per vote out of his own pocket to buy a governorship. And the disgrace, to cite a general reality, is the overwhelming power of incumbent congressmen to get re-elected. There's something fundamentally wrong when, even in a bad year for incumbents, 93 percent of House members seeking re-election get re-elected.

Our real purpose should not be to view politics as a gladiatorial contest between two ambitious people. Politics should be the process by which the country talks to itself about its future, a politics powered by a public that is reasonably informed about the candidates on the levels at which it decides to vote. Measured against that standard, we have a pitifully discouraging system because, in part, we are starving it to death.

Compare the amount of money we spend on politics with what Coca-

Cola or General Motors spends on advertising. We spend more of our national income telling ourselves what to drink and what to drive than we do on deciding our political destiny. Politics is, after all, the zone in which we discuss the management of a free society. And there's a tendency to confuse what's spent on government with what's spent on politics. But money spent on government goes for bureaucracy, while money spent on politics determines what kind of political management this society will have. Any corporation which spent, as a percentage of its total economic activity, the same portion on management as our society does on politics would go bankrupt.

A free society needs a free competitive system. I have far more faith in private dollars freely given by free citizens to the PACs that will be their watchdogs than I do in any kind of public financing of congressional campaigns. If the congressman whom you distrust because he will be "corrupted" by PACs would be in charge of a public financing system, why would you trust that public financing system?

The challenge for the eighties is to steadily increase the relationship between a person's vote and the behavior of the government. PACs are a strong and healthy step in that direction. We need more not fewer.

It's a tribute to the American Medical Association and the American Society of Association Executives that they have produced a publication which puts political action committees in their proper historical perspective. The title—"A Nation of Associations"—sums it up well.

Acknowledgements

Seldom are volumes written without the inspiration and guidance of others. The Honorable Newt Gingrich, Member of the House of Representatives from Georgia, asked the indispensable question: why have the adherents of political action associations failed to meet the challenge of their opponents—especially in the marketplace of ideas—and to present an up-beat but scholarly account of their role in the American political system? Knowing well that "ideas have consequences," Mr. Gingrich not only asked the question, but, in addition, gave others to believe that an intellectual defense was possible. Among those listening to his message was Linda Hudson, of the American Medical Political Action Committee. Her understanding of the theoretical-practical dimensions surrounding the future of political committees led her to conceive the project that resulted in this book. Her cheer, enthusiasm and energy nourished the work; and she provided a continual source of encouragement plus an occasional but always tactful "nudge" when the circumstances so required. The American Medical Political Action Committee showed foresight and boldness in providing assistance to a project involving one of the thorniest issues of the time. Their support, kindness, and good wishes should serve as a model to other political committees.

Good words are also in order for the American Society of Association Executives, for readily embracing this manuscript, and agreeing to publish it. Thanks to ASAE's volunteer leaders, to James P. Low, CAE, President of ASAE, and to Elissa Matulis Myers, CAE, for their substantial contribution to the publication of this book.

Benjamin Scott Waldman participated in nearly every stage leading to this volume; his assistance cannot be measured by this brief acknowledgement. Stuart Anderson did preliminary research on the history of voluntary associations. Daniel Addison worked especially hard and without complaint.

The faculty and staff of the Rose Institute of State and Local Government provided me with a home during the writing of this manuscript. Dr. Alan Heslop, its Director, offered me a critical eye, numerous thoughtful hours, and continuous support.

Acknowledgements

[illegible]

[illegible]

[illegible]

[illegible]

Section I
Introduction

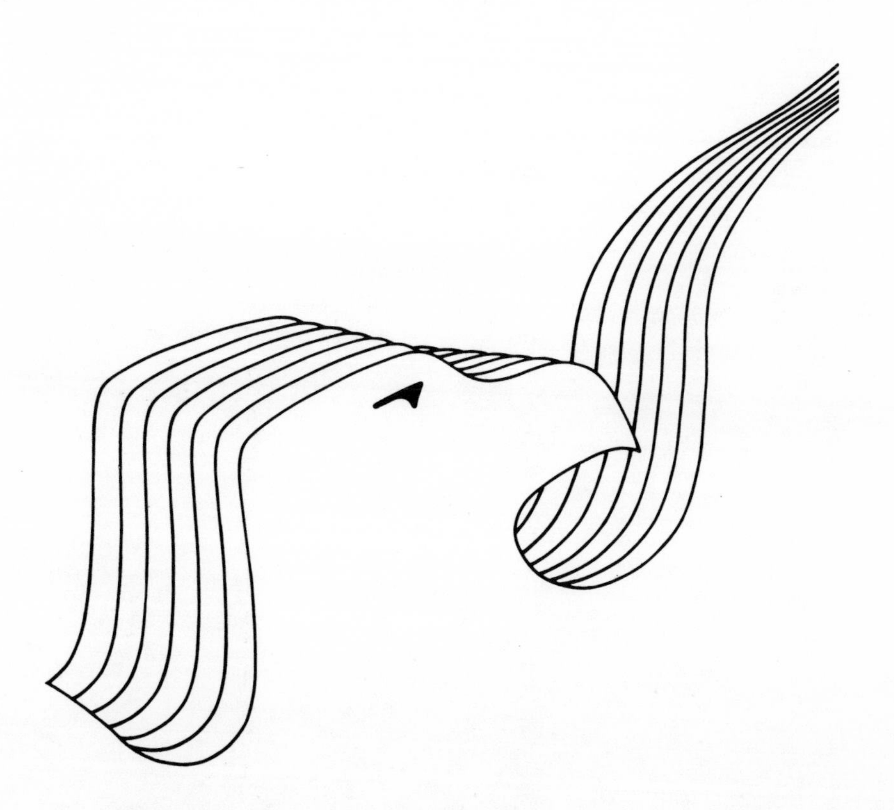

Introduction

The morals and intelligence of a democratic people would be in as much danger as its commerce and industry if ever a government wholly usurped the place of private associations.

Alexis de Tocqueville

Political Associations: An American Tradition

Perhaps no institution of contemporary American politics is more controversial and less understood than the political action committee. In its present form it was ushered into being by the Federal Election Campaign Act of 1971, the 1974 Amendments to the FECA, the 1974 Sun Oil decision by the Federal Elections Commission, and the 1976 decision by the United States Supreme Court in *Buckley v. Valeo.* Although the scope of its activities and its organizational structure are the result of federal law and interpretation, present-day political action committees play a role in the political system that dates to colonial America. Political action associations are inseparable from the political history of the United States—a form of voluntary organization whose members associate of their own will to advance shared interest and principle. As such, they are wholly consistent with the spirit and letter of democracy—indeed, they embody a creative expression of the democratic ideal, constituting an intermediate state of organization and representation between the mass of citizens and the various levels of government. These nongovernmental yet authoritative entities serve to contribute their member's resources to candidates for public office, and to support programs of political education.

Of these two functions, both the critics and the adherents of political committees agree that the former is more significant than the latter. In short, then, PACs constitute one of the sources of money in politics—an embarrassing subject to many, but a topic of critical importance to a self-governing people. The importance of the subject is suggested by the following. Although the political action committee operates in the full light of law, the introduction of private dollars into the electoral process continues to generate emotional responses and a host of critics committed to making government the principal, if not the sole, source of money in politics. Thus, the controversy surrounding political action committees is not simply over money in politics; rather, it represents competing conceptions of a free society, including the question, are the conditions of freedom better secured through private or public action?

Nowhere in the controversy have the really important questions been raised—at best, there are only glimpses of them amidst the charges emanating from competing camps. For instance, some of the critics of political associations hold them to be a corruption of the public interest, if not of democracy itself. Their adherents, by contrast, tend to identify with them as a mere instrument of self- or group-interest or of single-issue advocacy. Although a debate of national dimension is now taking place, critics and adherents appear to share little common ground, other than a sense of apprehension, if not danger, about the future of these associations.

Indeed, the parties to the controversy seem to be "talking past" one another, addressing different audiences, speaking to different concerns, and indulging in assertion and hyperbole, rather than in reason and careful argument. At best, they dwell on such mechanical questions as how many "PAC dollars" were given to how many candidates in the last election. This is not meant to suggest that this order of question is inappropriate or inconsequential to the debate. In fact, it is partly the purpose of the present study to raise these questions, seeking clarity in light of their underlying assumptions and their implications for public policy. More important, however, is the need to raise the question of principle—the role and function of private political associations in a free society. Without a full and systematic discussion of this critical question, a just and lasting understanding of the place of political action committees within the electoral process must remain beyond reach. This is the primary purpose of the following pages.

Although the parties to the debate have failed to address the relationship of private political associations to the framework of American democracy (at best they have advanced certain assumptions, grounded less in theory, history, and practice than in ideology, interest, and emotion), the point of departure for such an investigation is less complex than it may first appear. The political action committee is a form of political association, itself an elaboration of the long established tradition of voluntary associations in the United States. This tradition has been the fruitful topic of almost all commentaries on American democracy, although nowhere has it received a more penetrating, comprehensive, and insightful treatment than in Alexis de Tocqueville's *Democracy in America.*

Traveling in America in 1830, Tocqueville observed that "Americans of all ages, all stations of life, and all types of disposition are forever forming associations. There are not only commercial and industrial associations in which all take part, but others of a thousand different types—religious, moral, serious, futile, very general and very limited, immensely large and very minute."[1] Separating voluntary associations into two categories, civil and political, Tocqueville had noticed one of the characteristic features of American life—a feature that had no institutional counterpart among the nations of Europe. The conclusion he drew from this basic observation was simple and direct: "In countries where such associations do not exist, if private people do not artificially and temporarily create something like them, I see no other dike to hold back tyranny of whatever sort, and a great nation might with impunity be oppressed by some tiny faction or by a single man."[2]

Tocqueville understood, perhaps better than anyone before or since, the importance of voluntary and cooperative action to the maintenance of a free society. Where voluntary associations are weak, he argued, government grows strong. Where people do not share a common heritage of civil associations, government steps in to perform even the ordinary activities of daily life. In the process, individual liberty all but disappears. Political associations in particular check the designs of potential despots, ambitious minorities, and the tyranny of the majority. All aspire to aggrandize power at the expense of individuals, groups, classes and genuine majorities, usurping the liberty of the people by enlarging the operations of government. The consequences of this, Tocqueville concluded, lead government to react with "instinctive abhorrence" toward political associations, seeking to check their activities, including those that aim "to make some political opinion triumph, to get some politician into government, or to snatch power from another."[3]

Although Tocqueville elevated voluntary associations into a principle of freedom, they had in fact been a feature of American life since the founding of the colonies. Indeed, voluntary associations that dot the American landscape today are heirs to a living tradition, now almost four hundred years old, that has formed the character of American social and political behavior, and has significantly contributed to the maintenance of a free society and free political institutions.

The Debate Defined

What was commonplace in 1830—in fact, commonplace throughout the course of American history—has today become a subject of dispute. Indeed, it often seems that the traditional suspicion and hostility that characterized the outlook of European governments towards political associations increasingly inform the attitude of two classes of Americans: namely, public officials, and those who undertake to shape and influence public opinion. If the focus of the debate is the political action committee, the perspective from which its opponents assert their claims is "opposition to special interests." For instance, Congressman David Obey read into the *Congressional Record* an editorial from the Watertown, South Dakota *Public Opinion,* citing a Common Cause study of the influence and ambitions of political action committees. The editorial concludes on the following note:

> ... *Common Cause believes the time may have come for citizens "to reclaim their government" and invoke stringent curbs on the activities of special interest groups devoted to obtaining congressional action benefitting only themselves.*[4]

Watertown is not an isolated example. Editorials have appeared in the *New York Times* and in the *Washington Post* bearing the same tone. They have also appeared in the *Stockton Record* in California, in the *St. Petersburg Times* in Florida, and in innumerable other national and local newspapers. Their indictment against "political action committees for special interests"[5] runs the gamut from mere mischievousness to significant injury to the democratic process.

One editorial claims that contributions from political committees are "one of the root causes of the fragmentation of Congress in recent years. Members become less dependent on and less responsible to party principles, party programs, and party leadership." The same editorial, quoting Vice President Walter Mondale, states that special interest money is responsible for the lack of "trust" by the American voter in a system that responds more to "millions of dollars pouring out every day" than to the average citizen.[6] Several editorial writers have asserted that political action committees benefit only the few at the expense of the people, and that, in fact, they distort the political process by erecting dollar barriers between the people and their elected representatives. Many have become particularly alarmed that PACs are exercising excessive electoral influence—indeed, may be "purchasing" elections, as the result of the significant increase in "corporate PAC" contributions since 1974. This fact, of course, gives rise to the almost universal accusation that "PAC dollars" corrupt, or potentially corrupt, elected officials. One form in which this allegation appears is that special interest money purchases favors, blocks the legislative agenda of the people, and enhances the power of entrenched incumbents, vesting unusual authority in select senior members, partly as the result of their ability to direct the resources of political committees to their colleagues. Finally, some writers argue that contributions from political action organizations favor incumbents, adversely affecting open competition between candidates and parties in legislative districts. Others, by comparison, suggest that special interest money from ideologically oriented, single-issue associations provides challengers with an unfair advantage, when they embrace such causes as "pro-life," environmental concerns, national security, and the rights of gun owners. These are formidable charges, and will be evaluated in the fourth section on public policy. It should be noted, however, that they all play on the notion of "special interests"—a term that has powerfully shaped the current debate.

Indeed, no term is more frequently heard in the debate over the future of political action committees than "special interest." Usually identified with the influence that money—and especially corporate money—is alleged to exert over the political system, no term has received less attention as to its definition and meaning, or is used more recklessly. In the print and broadcast media, in respectable journals, even in scholarly textbooks and treatises, special interests are spoken of as if they are the invisible hand of our political life and the principle source of political corruption. Even where commentators and editorial writers show moderation and balance, the very term "special interest" is used to suggest a force opposed to the general interest or common good. In fact, the term is often used in contradistinction to the most popular and frequently used word in the vocabulary of democratic politics, the "people." It also conjures such metaphors as "bigness" and omnipotence, as compared with the average man or "little guy," who is perceived to be relatively uninfluential in a mass society. These metaphors suggest, however unarticulated, the notion that special interests abridge the standard of equality, and violate the rules of fair play and the canons of justice. In part, the opponents of political action committees are succeeding in the debate because they have intimidated their adversaries with the label "special interest."

Although some critics identify special interests with anti-democratic motives, the very arguments they use to indict their adversaries frequently betray their own biases, offending in their own way the democratic canons of fairness and equality. For instance, the detractors of special interests often fail to include within that category labor unions—although union committees have typically contributed more per election than corporate committees. Most professional organizations, such as groups of educators, are not listed as special interests—although doctors, according to many critics, have erected in the American Medical Political Action Committee one of the most offending of all special interests. Single-issue interest groups, including environmentalists, women's organizations, and minority associations escape the special interest label—although not, need it be said, Gun Owners of America. This form of discrimination is often so blatant that "public interest," "good government" groups such as Common Cause, the League of Women Voters, and Congress Watch are seemingly beyond reproach—although the National Legal Center for the Public Interest practices "special interest law," because it stands with the small businessman against the Occupational Safety and Health Administration.[7] A *New York Times* editorial speaks of "political action committees for special interests,"[8] thus subtly distinguishing between political committees that serve narrow, self-interested motives, and those that serve broader, perhaps more altruistic causes. It is unfortunate that the editorial writer went on to focus on the "PAC problem" without adumbrating the moral and political partition separating "special interest" from "non-special interest" political associations.

In short, many of the adversaries of special interests manifest a "good guy, bad guy" mentality—a mentality that frequently tends to reflect hostility to the system of business enterprise. Their arguments silently pit the profit motive against the public interest, leaving the impression that those who associate with free enterprise and the private sector should not, as a result of their association, possess the same "right to influence" as others whose avowed dedication is to the public sector. Their use of the term "special interest" also leaves the impression that public officials are infinitely corruptible (although the generally proposed solution to this problem—public financing of election campaigns—would surrender the regulation of our electoral machinery to the very same corruptible officials).

This points to another bias of the critics of special interests. Not only is their hostility aimed at the system of private profits, but, in addition, it is frequently directed against the private sector generally. Their arguments almost always manifest a "statist" mentality. They seek to substitute government regulation, if not preemption, for private and voluntary action in the political arena—as, for example, the proposal for public financing. The same *New York Times* editorial cited above suggests the ultimate intention of at least one influential critic: "If Congress won't establish public financing of campaigns as a substitute for PAC dollars, at least let it restrict the rising influence of PAC money and PAC pressure. *There'll be time later to drop the other shoe.*"[9] There is no little irony in the fact that those who are predisposed to public sector solutions often fall silent about the influence wielded in the electoral and legislative process by other powerful vested interests (or should those, too, be called "special interests"?), such as elected officials, bureaucrats, and those who are materially advantaged by government largesse.

It is unfortunate that these biases should have permeated the arguments of so many critics. Their presence in the debate is a disservice to truth, and significantly hinders an open and intelligent public discussion of a vital area of public policy and democratic principle. Political action committees do, of course, exercise considerable influence. A democracy that would avoid open and candid deliberation about such a formidable presence necessarily imperils its integrity, let alone its existence. Yet ideologically charged arguments and language only serve to prevent the democracy from considering its real problems, and, willy-nilly, provoke emotionalism, anxiety, and rigid doctrinal reactions on the part of all parties to the dispute.

The adherents of political action committees have performed little better in the debate than have the critics. On the whole, they have maintained a defensive posture, reacting—often at a late moment—when attacked, and failing to present a positive picture of the role of political associations in fostering the greater good of American democracy. Yielding to their adversaries that they are indeed special interests, they tend to assert their rights in the name of interest rather than principle.

Moreover, they seem to believe that political action committees are unproblematic institutions, or that their emergence as a force in the political arena raises few if any legitimate questions. Their fondest hope seems to be that their critics and the public will forget about their existence, that they might be free to go about their "business as usual." When it is pointed out to them that between 1977-1978, corporate, professional, and trade association political action committees gave $12.0 million to incumbents in federal races as compared with only $3.7 million to challengers, they fall silent, often unwilling to admit that this portends a problem for the political process, as well as for the future of political associations.

That the adherents of political committees have been unwilling to mount an adequate defense or offense skews the current debate, and permits their enemies to freely substitute emotionalism and ideology for rigorous argument. This also explains why the opponents of corporate committees have succeeded in identifying their opposition with the tag "special interests." It suggests, also, that business and professional committees do not dominate the political process—indeed, that the balance of influence is far from favoring them or the enterprise system. In fact, the adherents of political action committees will always be in retreat until they recognize that the future of these associations belongs, as with so many important issues of public and social policy, to whomever has the most persuasive arguments and the most effective means of reaching public opinion. The opponents of political committees have succeeded as well as they have because they command the marketplace of ideas—largely as a result of default. And although it is not always true that good ideas drive out bad, the prospects for a compelling and successful defense of political associations are today especially good given the opposition of public opinion to the further intrusion of government into the lives and the workplaces of the American electorate.

Purpose of the Present Study

That the adversaries of political action committees have so far gained the initial advantage in the debate over the future of this form of political association is both a problem and a subject for some reflection. In part their advantage is due to the complacency of those who, taking the tradition of voluntary associations for granted, have allowed their opponents to carry the argument to their front stoop. After all, what was once thought by Europeans to be a unique feature of American democracy has become over the course of time part of the marrow of our national life. What is now taken for granted, however, was once novel, vital, and inspiring—part of the belief of the Founding Fathers that American social and political institutions held the promise of securing liberty against the tyranny of one man or of many men. The purpose of this study is to examine the political action committee in light of precendents drawn from American history and political thought, and to recapture the meaning and intention of the tradition of voluntary associations, so that later generations can understand, articulate, and enjoy the way of life which, although now into the second century of the republic, continues the promise of its Founders.

FOOTNOTES

[1] Alexis de Tocqueville, *Democracy in America,* Volume II, Part 2, Chapter 5

[2] Tocqueville, Volume I, Part 2, Chapter 4

[3] Tocqueville, Volume II, Part 2, Chapter 7

[4] Hon. David R. Obey, *Congressional Record,* September 21, 1971, p. E4688

[5] Obey, p. E4687

[6] Obey, p. E4688

[7] Steven D. Lydenberg, *Bankrolling Ballots: The Role of Business in Financing Campaigns,* pp. 1, 69-71

[8] "How to Stop Ducking the PAC Problem," *New York Times,* September 21, 1979

[9] *Times,* September 21, 1979

Section Two
The Theory of Voluntary Associations

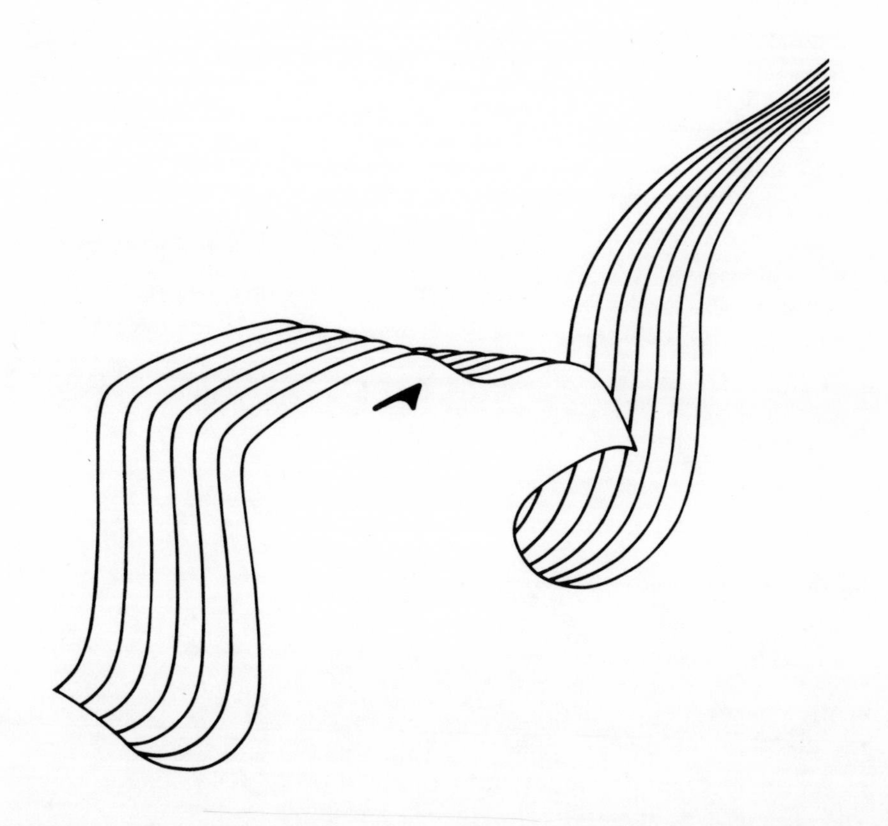

Chapter One
Background

The history of voluntary associations in America dates to the seventeenth century and is as old as the first permanent English colonies in North America. Although the tradition of associations originally stems from a set of religious beliefs transported by the Massachusetts Bay Puritans to the New World, the development of a multiplicity of civil and political associations soon followed. Indeed, the associational impulse was being felt before the American Revolution. And while the proliferation of voluntary associations is more characteristic of the nineteenth and especially the twentieth centuries, by comparison with Europe, eighteenth century America blossomed with them.

The success of voluntary associations has made them appear indigenous to the society which gave them birth, and almost "second nature" to the people whose identity is shaped by participation in them. The causes of their existence are numerous, and include, besides the Puritan religious heritage and the Constitutional emphasis on associations of interest, several accidental or historical causes. For example, the development of this tradition was accelerated by the distance between the government in London and the English colonies of North America some three thousand miles away. At best, the power of royal government was weakly exercised by colonial governors, and even proprietary colonies could barely maintain rule over rapidly expanding populations and the opportunities presented by an ever-expanding frontier. The absence of a strong governmental presence favored attitudes of self-reliance, self-government, and voluntary action, including political action, for common purposes. These attitudes were re-enforced by the lack of such feudal institutions as primogeniture, a titled nobility, a monopoly of religious authority by one church, standing armies, and guilds. Without those traditional structures and practices that in Europe influenced or regulated the social, economic, and political life of the people, it seemed natural to Americans to "test the waters," and then to exercise their own will over a relatively uninhibited environment. Indeed, the American environment added another critical factor to the development of an associational tradition. For those who had the endurance to challenge an unsettled continent, the absence of old world institutions and ways and the reality of a great expanse of land and opportunity left individual and community initiative as almost the only touchstone for survival, and for obtaining goods sought in America.

Of course, the existence of available, abundant, and unregulated space was a primary attraction of North America for many communities that settled here during colonial times. Often united by some combination of religious, national, ethnic, and class interest, whole communities sought a place where their particular association could prosper in peace according to its own ways. These hardy folk frequently composed both a communion and a community, and, thus, were organized voluntarily from within, not shaped and maintained from above by artificial structures. The strength of voluntary associations as an American custom has much to do with habits engendered by the colonial experience.

As democracy in America deepened and broadened throughout the nineteenth and twentieth centuries, voluntary associations were adapted to meet new needs, from movements for moral regeneration to organizations created to address the industrialization of the nation. And although many voluntary associations were generated by the absence of government—especially in colonial America—just as many if not more developed in response to the intrusion of government. If trade and professional associations developed in the eighteenth century in the absence of guilds and mercantilist economic policies, they developed in the nineteenth and twentieth centuries as a response to government exercising guild-like powers over what had hitherto been a free economic environment. Other associations that sprang into being as a response to government intervention were the Sons of Liberty in the 1760's, the grange movement in the latter decades of the nineteenth century, and the emergence of union, corporate, trade, and professional political committees in the twentieth.

The line separating civil and political associations often faded during these centuries as groups organized entirely for moral, religious, social, or economic motives found themselves in conflict with government or with other associations that sought to command government advantage for their own ends.

Always, however, the response was the same: Common action aimed at government, elections, and public opinion. Thus, although a tradition of associations was stimulated by the absence of government in colonial America, the pattern of free, collective organization to effect mutual interest or principle had become so deeply embedded in the consciousness of Americans, that it became "the first line of defense" against potential or actual government intrusion. Indeed, because voluntary association is so natural a response by Americans to almost any problem, government itself has sometimes created associations or shaped their form, including those that seek to influence public officials—as, for example, the contemporary political action committee.

Chapter Two
The *Federalist* and the Mythology of Special Interests

The discussion of the origin and development of voluntary associations in America cannot begin without reference to the era of the writing and ratification of the United States Constitution. The founding of the American republic is an event that sheds light on everything before and after it in our history. Those were seminal years, for they involved not only significant actions, but, in addition, national deliberation about the origin, function, and purpose of civil society and government. Rarely in the history of the world has a people reflected on and debated such profound questions—questions that go to the very meaning of what it is to be a man and a citizen.

A principal document guiding the debate of 1787–1788 was the *Federalist.* Although its authors, James Madison, Alexander Hamilton, and John Jay, were relatively young men—Hamilton was only thirty, Madison thirty-six, and Jay forty-two—their practical and theoretical judgment was sufficient to convert their work into what many consider to be the classic commentary on the Constitution, even the most significant American contribution to the history of political thought. The nation has changed much since 1788, yet the political principles to be found in the eighty-five papers comprising the *Federalist* retain a remarkable vitality for the America of the 1980's.

At the very heart of its teaching about republican government is the concept of self-interest—a topic that, under the rubric of "special interests," is at the center of the controversy over political action committees. The role of private interest or self-interest in economic and political life had always been a controversial subject. Madison and Hamilton knew well that to elevate individual and group interest into a principle of government would be a novel, if not a bold, undertaking. Indeed, the history of political thought from ancient Greece to the early modern world gave strong support to the position that the self-interest motive creates rivals and antagonists out of fellow citizens, threatening the unity of opinion and purpose on which the harmony of democratic societies rests. It was commonly believed that it nurtures greed and ambition, sowing in the very offices of government instability and disorder and finally culminating in tyranny.

Madison and Hamilton did not entirely disagree with this evaluation. Unimpeded, self and group interest, they believed, are destructive of the rights of others and of the continuing and total interests of any society. They also believed, however, that self and group interest are "sown into the nature of man."[1] To deny the legitimate role of self-interest in the operations of the economy and polity is offensive to the natural tendency of men, once freed of governmentally imposed restraints, to pursue their economic, social, and political well being. The effort to remove or limit its influence as a cause of human behavior is therefore tantamount to tyranny.

In their construction of the American Union, Madison and Hamilton sought to control the deleterious consequences of individual and group interest, yet to provide for a society that would allow the free play of the self-interest motive—indeed, for an economy and government that would be energized by its competitive and dynamic quality. On this, they believed, turned the freedom and prosperity of its citizens. (*Federalist* #10 summarizes this unprecedented experiment. "The regulation of these various and interfering interests involves the spirit of party and faction in the necessary and ordinary operations of the government."[2])

If self-interest is the lightning rod of free societies, it also constitutes their greatest threat. Self-interest undermines the very liberty that sustains its operation when it becomes a source of faction—the point at which individual interests become "united and actuated" by their association with other, similar interests, and then pose a threat to "the rights of other citizens or to the permanent and aggregate interests of the community."[3] Indeed, it is not faction simply, but rather the "mischiefs of faction" and the "violence of faction" that most concern Hamilton and Madison. The *Federalist,* then, distinguishes between those groups that are intent upon inflicting harm upon others for their own particular ends, and those that have learned the practice of conciliation and compromise. It is the latter that the authors of the *Federalist* wish to nurture, and the former, whether they be religious, ideological, or economic, whose effects they seek to blunt. By no means, however, do they intend to subvert or set aside the natural operation of interests, private or group, in the economic, social, and governmental spheres.

By comparison with the approach of the *Federalist,* the contemporary treatment of the self-interest concept appears narrow, rigid, and doctrinaire. Consider, for example, Max McCarthy's treatment of special interests in his *Elections for Sale.*

> *In modern American political terms, a special interest group is just what the name implies—a group, organization, or association with special axes to grind and special favors to ask. The groups have narrow interests, as contrasted with the broader public interest... There is nothing inherently evil in all this. But their goals are not always consistent with the broader public interest.*[4]

In defining special interest, McCarthy establishes the distinction between "narrow," self-serving interests and the "public interest," and implies that the latter is the standard by which the former is to be judged. Who are these parochial groups? They include "corporations, organized labor, farmers, liberal and conservative groups, medical and health insurance associations, gun enthusiasts, environmental, peace, and national defense groups, and many more."[5] McCarthy's list is so complete that hardly an American voter does not qualify for membership in a special interest. How, then, is the public interest determined?

> *It is up to elected officials of the United States to weigh the many competing interests and desires and reach a balanced decision in the national interest and, indeed, in the interest of the survival of all mankind. No U.S. official should be beholden to one or a few groups. And no group or individual should have a greater claim on our elected leaders than any other.*[6]

The function of representative government, McCarthy argues, is to adjudicate the merits of competing interests, implying that it is the duty of elected officials to rise above the claims made against them. In short, he expects from democratically elected officials behavior that he would not expect of the people who help to elect them.

Just as McCarthy distinguishes between the higher duty of elected officials and the lower and narrower desires of competing interests, so too he distinguishes between self-serving particular interests and an ideal of the people with relatively homogeneous interests as defined by the "little man." Similar notions of a democratic community, united by bonds of shared interest, opinion, and passion, and endangered only by the greed and desire for power of select persons and groups, have played a significant role in twentieth century American political thought, and have had a major impact on our national life, including the reforms of the Progressive Era, the social and economic policies of the New Deal, and the radical movements of the 1960's. It is an idea that found its most important expression in the works of the eighteenth century French political philosopher, Jean Jacques Rousseau, and, above all, it embodies the desire for human equality.

According to Madison, however, the attempt to give to all citizens the same interests, opinions, and passions is antithetical to the spirit of a free people. In a society where the theory and practice of equality prevail, the people are at liberty to form their own opinions, interests, and associations, and, in fact, it is human nature to do so. For example:

> *The diversity in the faculties of men, from which the rights of property originate, is not less an insuperable obstacle to a uniformity of interests. The protection of these faculties is the first object of government. From the protection of different and unequal faculties of acquiring property, the possession of different degrees and kinds of property immediately results; and from the influence of these on the sentiments and views of the respective proprietors, ensures a division of the society into different interests and parties.*[7]

In the Middle Ages, property rights were defined by a complex set of social relationships serving the interest of three groups, the monarchy, the aristocracy, and the church. The talents and aspirations of most men were subject to these artificial hierarchies, condemning them to the rule of force, tradition, and superstition. Breaking with the past, Madison sought to root property rights in what is first or natural for men—in the "faculties" (abilities or talents) of different men to create property or to make property useful to others. Although different abilities and talents lead to "the possession of different degrees and kinds of property"—an admitted inequality of result—the purpose of government is to insure the fundamental equality by which all men, regardless of class, religion, origin, or race, reap the rewards that are the just result of their own endowments. The same vision of equality that permits each man to achieve his own level of success in the market place, of course, also gives rise to the freedom to unite and organize in associations to foster mutual interest.

The conclusion to which Madison is brought, then, is that in a free society the people will appear for all politically relevant purposes in the guise of associations of interest, seeking to enlarge the influence of their members, and expecting their elected representatives to advocate their causes. Furthermore, he makes no distinction between narrow, self-serving interests and those that avow a broader concern with mankind. Both are a cause of the division of society; both seek to command the public sphere, often at the perceived expense of the other. In this respect, all men are, or are potentially, members of one or another special interest—that is, an association partial to the interests of their group. The distinction between special interests vis-a-vis other forms of associations of interest is foreign to the lexicon of Madisonian politics.

Unlike McCarthy's ideal of a democratic society possessing homogeneous interests, Madison's ambition was to create a society with genuine differences of interest among its citizens. Such a society, Madison well knew, runs risks peculiar to itself. In one of the most telling accounts of what it means fully to embrace a society of associations based on interest, Madison writes:

> *And what are the different classes of legislators but advocates and parties to the causes which they determine? Is a law proposed concerning private debts? It is a question to which the creditors are parties on one side and the debtors on the other. Justice ought to hold the balance between them. Yet the parties are, and must be, themselves the judges; and powerful faction must be expected to prevail.*[8]

Madison's intention is not to legitimize injustice—conversely it is his profound belief that, "Justice is the end of government."[9] And although some "theoretical politicians" believe the relationship of democracy to justice is as simple as "reducing mankind to a perfect equality in their political rights,"[10] he knows it to be much more complex—indeed, perhaps the thorniest and most enduring of all the problems of politics. Rule by the people, Madison understands, is a double-edged sword. Resting on the principle of the equal rights of all men, democracy supports the liberty of individuals to associate for common interest; it also holds the potential, where interests conflict and where there is no source of authority outside of the people themselves, for one portion of the community to abuse the rights of another. In the case of maximum danger to the rights of others, majority faction, or tyranny, threatens the very equality from which the liberty of association originates.

Madison understood with remarkable clarity and candor almost unknown in political discourse today the implications of what it means for the people to govern themselves—including the possibility of democratic tyranny. Given the insights of his critique into this form of government, his intention, by comparison, is even more remarkable: to reaffirm faith in the capacity of men to govern themselves by building safeguards against the time when one portion of the community will seek to dictate public policy at the expense of the rights of others. In this respect, Madison and McCarthy share similar concerns about the influence of self- and group-interest over society and government. Similar concerns, however, lead to radically different approaches, both as to the analysis and to the solution of the problem.

The first point of difference between Madison and modern writers such as McCarthy is that the former believes it is not only select persons and groups who will seek to oppress the people, but also the "little man," who, feeling the strength of his interests and opinions in a truly democratic society, may seek to endanger the rights of individuals and minorities. In a free society, the "little man," perhaps out of envy or the lack of enlightenment, is just as likely to have designs on persons or groups who do not share his orientation as are those who seek to preserve or enhance their wealth, privileges, and special ways. The idea that the people, if undisturbed by the corrupting influence of greedy or power-hungry interests, are essentially "good," has no standing in the political thought of James Madison. Neither, however, does Madison argue that the people are "evil." Rather, his view is a balanced one, not partaking of any extreme. In a closely related thought, Alexander Hamilton suggests that "the supposition of universal venality in human nature is little less an error in political reasoning than the supposition of universal rectitude" [11]—a perspective that captures Madison's view of what it means to think about the question, "Who are the people?"

Another point of difference between Madison and McCarthy is the full scope and range Madison gives to the play of interest in society and government. Madison sought to create a society in which a multiplicity of competing interests, inserting themselves into the very counsels of the political and governmental process, will check the probability that select groups would dominate the decision making process. Although regretting to some extent the need to elevate, and thus to dignify self-interested motives, Madison nevertheless legitimizes the role of interest in the political and governmental arenas as the most efficacious check on the possibility of tyranny. McCarthy, by contrast, admits the existence of such interests but would then proceed to limit their scope and influence on the offices of government. McCarthy suggests that legislators, if unimpeded by special interests, are able to transcend self-seeking motives, directing their efforts to the true interests of the people and to the national interest. By contrast, Madison believes that elected officials will be no better than the people who elect them, and that in a truly free society, given the appropriate institutional safeguards, restraints and incentives, the admission of a multiplicity of interests into the electoral and governmental process is the best check against the tyranny of one man, a few men, or of many men. It is also a check against those who, believing that men can live beyond interest—as if "men were angels" or "angels were to govern men" [12]—seek to remake society in the name of the people along some utopian ideal.

In the light of McCarthy's views, Madisonian thought initially appears selfish, if not sinister. Nothing that has been said so far, however, should be taken to suggest that Madison's political philosophy is devoid of a conception of the general interest of society. Above all, that interest is contained in the Preamble to the United States Constitution, and includes the creation of a more perfect union, the establishment of justice, the insurance of domestic tranquility, provisions for the common defense, the promotion of the general welfare, and the securing of the blessings of Liberty now and in the future. The greatest threat to these grand objectives, Madison believed, was the unfettered pursuit of self- and group-interest. Thus, rather than frustrating the role of interest, Madison proposes to employ it against itself, freeing it, encouraging groups to become more numerous, and making self-interest respectable by giving it standing within the very operations of a democratic-republic. Madison did not wish legislators to be "beholden" to powerful or not so powerful interest groups. Furthermore, he did not expect the decision making process to turn exclusively or simply on the demands of interest groups. Rather, he sought to admit the influence of associations of interest into the structures of politics and government, knowing that among a free people, the general interest, including the blessing of liberty, cannot be sustained other than by involving those narrower interests that compose the economic and social existence of the citizenry.

Without shame or apology, Madison builds republican institutions in America on the principle of self- and group-interest. He saw in the admission of a multiplicity of interests into the political and governmental arena the strongest check against the selfishness and, thus, the tyranny of one man, a few, or many men. For if the problem of democratic politics is the propensity of men to form into associations of interest, advocating their concerns to the detriment of the rights of others, Madison's solution is to multiply such associations, thwarting the likelihood that one or a few interests will dominate the government and, thereby, the whole of society.

The principal objective of the *Federalist,* it must be remembered, was the defense of a new union of the states under a government of radically different proportions than existed under the Articles of Confederation. Its account, therefore, of voluntary associations takes place within the context of an explanation regarding the origin and purpose of government, and the principal threat to republican government—"faction." Unlike Marxists who believe in a classless, stateless utopia, the authors of the *Federalist* believed in the "indispensable necessity of government."[13] For Marx, the critical problem of political life is class conflict. Class conflict is both the source of historical change and the justification for government. The abolition of classes, in turn, leads to the "withering away" of the state, and finally, according to the Marxist theory, to a transformation of the human condition, now freed of the conventions that are the root of its vices.

The *Federalist* also teaches that "faction" (a major source of which is class conflict) is the cause of government. Faction divides society into competing interests, each seeking satisfaction at the expense of the rights of others. As long as men enjoy the freedom to pursue their interests and to form associations to advance them, Madison argues in the 10th *Federalist,* government will be required to hold the balance between competing parties.

Faction, then, is the fundamental reality of political life, and its strength comes from the fact that it is rooted in human nature. Faction gives rise to the need for government, and, by the same token, suggests the permanence of associational activity as the primary vehicle for expressing man's deepest needs, desires, and beliefs. The *Federalist* gives political associations a standing in the universe of political life that stems from the impulses of human nature itself. According to this view, political associations are not merely the result of historical accident but, rather, where men are free, associations necessarily arise as a condition of politics. Today this view is mirrored in the beliefs and practices of Americans. The freedom to associate, it is commonly thought, is almost always the first response of any body of citizens confronted with a problem of political dimensions.

The difference between Marx and Madison is that Marx holds government to be the subject of history, and class conflict to be the fundamental source of historical change. Historical change, Marx believes, makes possible a radical transformation of the human condition. Madison, to the contrary, argues that class conflict is only one among many other sources of faction, including "A zeal for different opinions concerning religion, concerning government," and "an attachment to different leaders ambitiously contending for preeminence and power." [14] Madison contends, moreover, that government is the subject of human nature: "But what is government itself, but the greatest of all reflections on human nature?" [15]

Madison's conception of the human personality is more complex and more penetrating than Marx's one dimensional account of man. In part this explains Marx's belief in the possibility of a classless, stateless society, and by comparison, Madison's realism, including his moderate approach to the solution of the problem of faction. The Marxist understanding of the human condition contributes to the notion, much in vogue today, that the people, if undisturbed by bothersome entities such as political associations, share homogeneous interests and wish only to be left to themselves—reflecting their existence in the hoped for world of complete communism. It also contributes to the idea that people can live without intermediary associations between themselves and government, and to the hoped for withering away of such associations in a society dedicated to altruistic, rather than self-interested, motives.

Although Madison initially identifies political associations with faction as the source of the problem of politics, he assigns them a function in the constitutional order that elevates them into something beyond a merely negative force. His solution to the problem of faction is to turn faction against itself, seeking to check its harmful effects by cultivating its numbers.

> *In a free government the security for civil rights must be the same as that for religious rights. It consists in the one case in the multiplicity of interests, and in the other in the multiplicity of sects. The degree of security in both cases will depend on the number of interests and sects; and they may be presumed to depend on the extent of country and number of people comprehended under the same government.*[16]

According to this account, the establishment of a more perfect union is the condition for increasing the number of interests that operate as a check on the effects of factious groups. Not only is the proliferation of interests to be promoted in society but, in addition, it is to play a critical role in government as well. "The regulation of these various and interfering interests forms the principal task of modern legislaton, and involves the spirit of party and faction in the necessary and ordinary operations of the government."[17]

Earlier we saw how McCarthy admits to the existence of a pluralistic society, but stops short when it comes to admitting the constellation of interests into the counsels of government. Why Madison insists upon their admission is the subject for the remainder of this discussion of the *Federalist*, and requires that we return to the general intentions of its authors as our point of departure.

Although it is common to think of America as a nation still in its youth, in truth it has existed longer under one form of government than any other nation in the modern world. As we anticipate the bi-centennial of the United States Constitution, we might reflect on the fact that to live nearly two hundred years under the same form of government is an accomplishment almost unparalleled by any other people in world history. And although this fact may not be sufficiently appreciated by Americans today, it would have meant a great deal to the men who gathered in Philadelphia between May and September 1787 to draft a new Constitution. Uppermost in their minds was the sorry and short-lived history of all previous experiments in democratic government. According to the *Federalist* the history of democracy is a sordid one. Ancient Athens, the famed "cradle of democracy," retained its constitution for a brief thirty years, declining into anarchy and then into tyranny. Indeed, with one or two notable exceptions, the example of Athens represented the general tendency of democracies in the ancient world and in the Italian city-states of the Renaissance.[18] This blighted history, Hamilton and Madison suggest, was the result of a basic defect in the fabric of those societies: the pure democracies of Greece and Italy fell into conflict and finally into civil war as a result of the intense face-to-face rivalry between competing interests among the people.

The solution to this problem, they argue, is a system of representation extending over a continent-wide Union. Representative government is distinguished from direct or pure democracy by the fact that the people do not legislate for their needs directly but rather participate in the political system as electors. Government by representatives, then, removes the immediate conflict of interests from the body of the people, locating it in an assembly where more or less equal delegates must deliberate and act, not only for the interests of their own constituency, but for the nation as a whole. This responsibility introduces moderation and the spirit of compromise into the deliberations of the nation's elected officials.

Moreover, the extension of the sphere of republican government to encompass a Union of all the states enlarges the possibility that a "multiplicity of interests"—not just a few as existed in the city-states—will be represented in the national councils, thus providing a check against the potential tyranny of one man, a few, or many men. In the 10th *Federalist*, Madison writes:

> *The other point of difference is, the greater number of citizens and extent of territory which may be brought within the compass of republican than of democratic government; and it is this circumstance principally which renders factious combinations less to be dreaded in the former than in the latter. The smaller the society, the fewer probably will be the distinct parties and interests, the more frequently will a majority be found of the same party; and the smaller the number of individuals composing a majority, and the smaller the compass within which they are placed, the more easily will they concert and execute their plans of oppression. Extend the sphere and you take in a greater variety of parties and interests; you make it less probable that a majority of the whole will have a common motive to invade the rights of other citizens, or if such a common motive exists, it will be more difficult for all who feel it to discover their own strength and to act in unison with each other.*[19]

The theory of representation embraced by the United States Constitution treats the people, not as a homogeneous entity, but rather as splintered into a thousand different interests and associations. Indeed, it is through these various associations that the people gain their public identity, and present themselves both as electors and as advocates before government. In a sense, then, "the people" as a homogeneous entity with uniform interests do not exist in America. Rather, the people represent themselves on election day, in public forums and before their elected officials, in the guise of associations that exhibit their concerns and needs. The freedom to associate, therefore, is a critical element of the electoral process and the operation of government. Indeed, it is critical to the maintenance of the democratic experiment as understood by the American founders.

The importance the *Federalist* assigns to the role of voluntary associations within a representative system of government must not be underestimated. The secondary form of representation characterized by a nation of associations is the real solution to the problem of faction, and the operative mechanism animating the constitutional system.

According to the authors of the *Federalist*, the most "constant and durable" source of faction is class distinction—especially the distinction between the few and the many, the rich and the poor. Above all, of the many forms of faction that had affected the freedom and stability of the earlier attempts at democratic government, class warfare was never far from the surface of any conflict, and was a continual source of agitation among the people. It was Madison's and Hamilton's anticipation, however, that a capitalist economy—as opposed to a traditional agricultural economy—would encourage the development of many different kinds of interests, and would mix members of all classes in various associations of interest. This, then, would avert the most dangerous form of associational division—the conflict of the haves and have-nots.

The authors of the *Federalist* believed that the more centers of influence in society the more prosperous the nation, the freer the people, and the less chance of tyranny either of the few or of the many. It is often argued today by opponents of special interests that the Fortune 500 represents a threat to the democratic process as the result of wealth and influence. The critics offer government regulation or preemption as a replacement for corporate power. Madison, by contrast, believed 500 is better than one—especially if the principal source of influence is government. To involve a multiplicity of associations in the political and governmental process is to insure many competing power centers, and that unique dynamism and sense of energy that comes from conflicting and clashing interests.

Madison characterized this system as one of "opposite and rival interests,"[20] and argued that it pertains to both state and society. As to government, he thought it the very secret of "good government" as well as of free government. If one takes the meaning of democracy seriously, and if no artificial barriers are constructed to the free association of people as their opinions and interests dictate, then government itself will reflect those opinions and interests—indeed, they will be the subject matter of government's principal concerns and actions. Rather than seeking to curb such a development, Madison described a system under the Constitution that would freely admit the representatives of differing opinions and interests into the process of elections and legislation. Because the people are to associate for political purposes principally according to interests, maximum access must be guaranteed to interest groups both as to the electoral process and to government. By including interests within the very process of the political system, Madison sought to satisfy their legitimate requests while employing them against one another in order to check the unjustifiable demands of group and individual self-interest. In doing this, he also believed that the competition among interests would unleash the power of the private sector, driving the engine of American society forward into a dynamic future. It would also supply energy, vigor, and efficiency to government by making it sensitive to the needs of a forward-moving economy and society. Among other things, harnessing the power of clashing and conflicting interests would provide the energy that is part of the *Federalist* definition of "good government."

Moreover, in this arena of various and differing interests will be found the primary check on any one or two interests seeking to dominate the electoral and governmental system, undermining its democratic quality. It was from this arena, also, that Madison thought justice would emerge—as a consequence of the concessions and compromises that must of necessity result from the pressures of so many differing interests upon elected officials. To subject public officials to conflicting interests, therefore, was the crucial first step to good government.

If a system of "opposite and rival interests" was to characterize the new union created by the Constitution, then it must, in the first instance, be nurtured into existence. In 1787 America was overwhelmingly agricultural. It was the expressed hope of the authors of the *Federalist* that agriculture would gradually give way to a commercial economy, including not only "a landed interest," but also "a manufacturing interest, a mercantile interest, a moneyed interest, with many lesser interests."[21] Such an economy, it was believed, based principally on the free market model supplied by Adam Smith's *Wealth of Nations*, would generate and maintain a system of numerous and sharply defined interests. The American founders, however, were not mere disciples of Smith's political economy. They did believe in a free economy as a means of producing multiple centers of power and of obtaining individual prosperity. But they also believed in government and in the role of government as a regulator. Again, however, their understanding of this matter differs sharply from those today who advocate government regulation.

In *Federalist* #10, Madison speaks of "The regulation of these various and interfering interests forms the principal task of modern legislation, and involves the spirit of party and faction in the necessary and ordinary operation of the government." Three points must be made by way of explanation.

First, Madison believed that in modern or "civilized nations" there existed "permanent and aggregate interests of the community."[22] These interests, running the gambit from agriculture to manufacturing and from labor to management, were indispensable to the strength of a modern economy and, equally, to the maintenance of that multiplicity of interests that guarantees liberty. Madison embraced Adam Smith's teaching as much for its political effects as for its economic. Consequently, he believed that whenever any one interest or interests becomes so powerful as permanently to damage others it is the role of government to step in and right the balance.

Second, Madison laid down no hard and fast rules as to when government should act but, rather, believed it was a matter of prudential judgement according to time and place. On the whole, government should respect and limit its involvement in the economy, entering only when egregious circumstances required intervention. The benefit of the doubt should always be given to the private sector, and all deference should be paid to the institution of private property. On the other hand, he would surely have approved of antitrust regulation, and of government programs designed to advance one or another section of the economy under adverse circumstances. Madison would not have approved of a government whose regulatory and other actions seek to direct, control, or even guide the production of goods and services generally or within a given industry.

Third, if government was to be assigned a regulatory function, then those who might be regulated must have complete and full access to the political process. The founders provided government with a regulatory capacity over "various and interfering interests;" at the same time, however, they intended that these same interests must be able to express their point of view—to influence—"the necessary and ordinary operations of the government." To provide government the right of regulation, but to restrict the activities of those who might be regulated, offends the understanding of democracy as expressed by Madison in the *Federalist*.

The *Federalist* cannot be labeled politically "right" or "left." It was written at a time prior to the emergence of those opinions that are embraced today by "conservatives" and "liberals." More important, it has left an imprint on American political institutions and modes of thought that is far greater—and that contains greater implications for the outcome of freedom—than contemporary popular ideologies. Take, for instance, the notion of special interests. While those on the "left" tend to speak of them as a menace to society, and those on the "right" invoke them as sacrosanct entities, both parties fail to comprehend their appropriate role within the definition of republican government. Although it is the task of government to protect the faculties of men against discrimination, it cannot simply eradicate differences between the weak and the strong, or organize free citizens to pursue their interests, including their claims against government. For this men must associate. From this point of view, every interest is special, and each man, if not a member of a special interest, should become one.

In fact, only to the extent that one identifies with a special interest does the ordinary man gain relevance in the political process. Making use of an already existing tradition of voluntary associations, Madison sought to give it new meaning by making it the primary or pre-political vehicle underlying the political process. Rooting the political system in the very organization and arrangement of society itself meant a greater chance of success for democratic institution and practices. Among other things, it meant that democracy would correspond to the habits and customs of the people; that there would be meaningful, free flowing exchange among citizens in their communities and in the deliberations of government; that government participation in the political process, including the electoral process, would be limited, thus checking the possibility of tyranny.

The *Federalist* perspective differs from contemporary conservatism and liberalism in other respects. Believing in the "indispensable necessity of government," its authors were not idle dreamers who believed that "men were angels" or that "angels were to govern men;" rather, they were realists who sought to frame government "which is to be administered by men over men."[23] Of course, in dealing with men as they are, rather than as they might be transformed by the mind of some utopian philosopher, the founders defined the very essence of republican government. After all, what else is republican government but the rule of some men over other men, periodically but regularly elected from out of the great body of the people, and under laws that possess legitimacy and force as a result of being rooted in the consent of the governed. The realism of the *Federalist*, then, is in fact synonymous with idealism—with one of the greatest ideals known to man, the right of a people to be self-governing. Thus, if the *Federalist* speaks of the "indispensable necessity of government," the focus of its presentation is "good government."[24] Long before the Progressives, the League of Women Voters, or Common Cause "discovered" and embraced the good government theme, it was the subject of the United States Constitution.

For the authors of the *Federalist*, of course, good government means something quite different from the usage it has received in the twentieth century. Among other things, Madison and Hamilton did not identify good government with "political reform" as that term is currently understood—that is, with the effort to depoliticize the electoral and legislative process. They thought it undemocratic, if not a violation of human nature, to attempt to take the "politics out of government." Instead they sought to cultivate, refine, and utilize the natural inclination of man as a political animal, providing under a written constitution for a system that would check and redeploy the less desirable tendencies of human nature. For instance, writing in *Federalist* #51, Madison argues that "ambition must be made to counteract ambition" through a system of separation of powers. To seek to negate ambition, or to prevent ambitious men from gaining office, is an affront to the idea of the rule of men over men. By contrast, Madison believed that it was possible to fulfill the ambitions of political men and serve the public interest by identifying personal motives with constitutionally established powers of office. Madison's discussion of ambition is an imitation of his remedy for the problem of faction—to turn faction against itself by increasing the volume of competing and conflicting associations of interest.

The authors of the *Federalist* certainly did not believe that the solution to every problem of democracy—including the problem of political corruption—was to further "democratize" the system. Just as in a monarchy, where the greatest danger to civil society is the unfettered rule of one man, in a truly democratic society, they believed, the greatest danger to the people is the unchecked rule of the people over themselves. Thus, their solution to the problems of democratic politics was not simply to democratize the system as a solution to every problem; rather it was creatively to employ checks and balances within society and government. One of those checks is to permit the entry of private interest into public counsels, reminding government of the existence of opposite and rival powers.

It is fashionable today for both liberals and conservatives to speak of the public interest—the interest of the people—vis-a-vis the interests or power of government. Madison and Hamilton shared a different perspective on this problem. In a truly democratic society, the government reflects the interests of the people. If government errs, it may well be the result of the people erring against themselves. Thus, checks and balances introduce cautionary warnings, fostering, in turn, greater deliberation and the spirit of compromise in private and public measures.

The *Federalist* concern for good government was not, as it is today, for a government that is politically neutral or depoliticized, and that must justify its every act before an egalitarian understanding of democracy. Rather, its concern was for a government that was efficient, stable, orderly—and, above all, free. The *Federalist* wanted to provide the people, in a meaningful sense, with access to their government, and insure vehicles for their political participation that were effective, lasting, and true. Prior to the American experiment in self-government, the history of democracy had been a sordid affair. Madison, Hamilton, and Jay wished to overcome that reputation by designing not only a Constitution, but, in addition, a society that was capable of supporting and maintaining democratic institutions and practices as a result of the nation's way of life. To this end, they wedded the tradition of voluntary associations to the political process, organizing that process under the Constitution to provide maximum access of the people, through their associations, to the political system. They did not discriminate in favor of one particular interest in opposition to others. Rather, acting as "enlightened statesmen," they sought to leave to later generations a system that would maintain the balance between the "permanent and aggregate interests of the community."

FOOTNOTES

[1]*Federalist*, #10
[2]*Ibid.*
[3]*Ibid.*
[4]Max McCarthy, *Elections for Sale*, pp. 23-24
[5]*Ibid.*, p. 24
[6]*Ibid.*
[7]*Federalist*, #10
[8]*Ibid.*
[9]*Federalist*, #51
[10]*Federalist*, #10
[11]*Federalist*, #76
[12]*Federalist*, #51
[13]*Federalist*, #2
[14]*Federalist*, #10
[15]*Federalist*, #51
[16]*Ibid.*
[17]*Federalist*, #10
[18]*Federalist*, #9
[19]*Federalist*, #10
[20]*Federalist*, #51
[21]*Federalist*, #10
[22]*Ibid.*
[23]*Federalist*, #51
[24]*Federalist*, #1

Chapter Three
Jefferson and Jackson: The Rise of Political Parties

No discussion of voluntary associations would be complete without reference to the biggest and most exciting voluntary associations in America—political parties. For this we must turn to the figure of Thomas Jefferson.

The election of Jefferson to the Presidency of the United States has been called "the second American Revolution." Among the important features of the election was the triumph of the Jeffersonians (the origin of the present day Democratic Party) and the extinction of the Federalist Party as a force in American politics. The origin of the Jeffersonians goes back to the dispute, often fierce, between Hamilton and Jefferson, each of whom resigned from George Washington's administration to organize against the other. That dispute reached its bitterest pitch in the last half of John Adam's administration with the publication of the Virginia and Kentucky Resolutions. Those documents, one authored by Madison, the other by Jefferson, proclaimed that the Alien and Sedition Acts had exceeded the constitutional authority of the federal government. The Alien and Sedition Acts sought to control the impact of growing pro-French sentiment by the Adams government in the United States in order to avoid American involvement in a European War. The Virginia and Kentucky Resolutions not only answered the Alien and Sedition Acts, but, according to Professor Harry Jaffa, became the first party platform of the first political party.[1]

Jefferson had been dissatisifed with the Washington Administration shortly after taking up the post as the nation's first Secretary of State. In particular, he objected to the plan devised by Hamilton, the first Secretary of the Treasury, to put the nation on a firm financial footing and to develop its commercial potential. Jefferson alleged that the plan for a Bank of the United States was a means of bestowing benefits on a favored commercial class to the detriment of the great mass of American husbandrymen. Moreover, he believed that such benefits would widen the gap between rich and poor, creating antagonisms that might lead to the imposition of a commercial aristocracy in America. When Franklin Roosevelt attacked the "economic royalists" in the mid 1930's, he was doing little more than taking a page from the book of Thomas Jefferson, the founder of his party.

Jefferson had little use for the concept of interest group politics. From his perspective the role assigned to "interests" and "parties" by the *Federalist* was antithetical to his notion of a good society and of a good government. Jefferson favored a society that looked upon equality in terms of *fraternity and liberty*. Advocating a nation of "cultivators," he argued that a society based on manufacturing corrupted morals and undermined the virtue necessary for republican government. If self-government is limited government, he thought, then the people must possess those habits, customs, and opinions that would make them individually self-governing in the absence of governmental authority. In short, he wanted a homogeneous society capable of sustaining among its citizens a uniform attachment to principle.

Above all, he detested the idea of parties and interests that sought their own ends rather than the harmony of society. Jefferson's distaste for interests and parties was in part a reflection of that seventeenth- and eighteenth-century attitude towards parties and factions as the source of intrigue, conspiracy, and usurpation.[2] If Jefferson thought such groupings were the source of mischief and tyranny, the authors of the *Federalist* thought that they were necessary—"sown into the nature of man"—and, thus, sought to disarm them by way of employing them. Jefferson never fully embraced the idea of a commercial republic with its multiplicity of interests. Of course, Jefferson had no hand in the writing of the Constitution, or in the events leading to its ratification. He was at the French court as America's Ambassador.

Because Jefferson was not present during the drafting of the Constitution and the subsequent debate over its ratification, his greatest contribution to American politics after 1787-88 was the development of an extraconstitutional device, the Political Party. As a means of overcoming the Federalist program (not to be confused with the meaning of Federalist as in the *Federalist Papers*), Jefferson knit together a national organization, a Party platform, and a flag around which to rally—Jefferson himself. His enormous popular victory in 1800 witnessed the triumph of his cause, and stands as a tribute to his organizational and strategic ability. In his First Inaugural Address, he sought to heal the wounds that had previously divided:

> *Let us, then, fellow-citizens, unite with one heart and one mind. Let us restore to social intercourse that harmony and affection without which liberty and even life itself are but dreary things. And let us reflect that, having banished from our land that religious intolerance under which mankind so long bled and suffered, we have yet gained little if we countenance a political intolerance as despotic, as wicked, and capable of as bitter and bloody persecutions.... We have called by different names brethren of the same principle. We are all Republicans, we are all Federalists.*

Jefferson sought harmony, not simply as a stabilizing device of an election aftermath, but rather as a fundamental posture of democratic society. His common appeal to the Republicans (another name for the Jeffersonian Party) and the Federalists was in fact a call to reunite all Americans on the same ground of principle. The first political party in the United States was a Party to end all parties. This dimension of party government has reasserted itself in American politics from time to time in certain seminal elections, establishing a broad national consensus under which both parties operate.[3]

The attempt by Jefferson to diminish the role and influence of interest group politics represents a competing "moral" tradition to the Madisonian model of republican government. Throughout American history, these alternative conceptions of a free society have not only competed, but have mingled, forming the character and, perhaps, contradictions of the American way.

Jefferson's success was great, but it was only temporary. By 1806, the son of President John Adams, John Quincy Adams, became a member of the party that bore the name of his father's old enemy. By 1820 America was experiencing the "Era of Good Feelings." The election of James Monroe that year symbolized the existence of only one party in America. The disputed election of 1824, however, ended whatever good feelings in fact existed, elevating John Quincy Adams to the White House and leaving an embittered Andrew Jackson to bide his time, planning the triumph that would take place in 1828.

Jackson's organizational and strategic ability was no less than Jefferson's. The deadlock in the electoral college in 1824 threw the election for the presidency into the House of Representatives. Although in 1824 Jackson won the greatest number of popular votes cast, his three opponents in that election out-polled him. He was intent on making sure that nothing similar occurred in 1828. Setting about to create, or rather, to recreate the Democratic Party (the name changed from the Jeffersonians to the Democratic Party in the early 1800's), Jackson sought to insure a favorable outcome of the election in advance of election day.

Under Jackson, political parties gained the function and characteristics they possess today. The aim of a party is to forge a coalition prior to an election, thus determining the outcome of the election. This extraconstitutional feature of American politics is by now "second nature." In the years 1824-1828, however, it was a unique phenomenon. Jackson set about to organize people in communities and states in what must have been one of the greatest volunteer efforts in the history of North America. Along the way, he invented the idea of national nominating conventions and involved the people in the political process in a way that had hitherto been unknown in the United States.

Upon his election, he used government patronage—the "spoils system"—to secure the continued dedication of party workers, to keep his coalition "in place" for future elections, and to govern with the support of a formal majority in Congress. When the Whig Party organized during Jackson's first term, it not only provided America with a two party system, but it adopted many of the ways and practices of the Democrats. Thus, by the election of 1832, America had the two party system it knows today.

Although Jackson sought to rekindle the flame of Jeffersonianism, his appeal was not merely to cultivators. Rather, his coalition included farmers (who cultivated primarily for profit) and a rapidly expanding class of what would today be called small businessmen.[4] In other words, his coalition included the very elements of a commercial society, the development of which Jefferson sought to frustrate. From this point forward in American history the normal operation of the two party system would systematize the "spirit of party and faction in the necessary and ordinary operations" of electoral politics as well as of government. Jacksonian Democracy legitimized the role of interest group politics within the political process, building on an assortment of voluntary associations to produce a national coalition capable of winning elections and of governing.

In at least one respect, however, Jacksonian democracy did manage to recapture the spirit of the Jeffersonian attack on interest groups. In an editorial in the *Washington Globe*, dated September 8, 1832, the editor attacked the campaign contributions by the Bank of the United States (approximately $100,000) to the Henry Clay campaign. "If the Bank, a mere moneyed corporation, can influence and change the results of our election at pleasure, nothing remains of our boasted freedom except *the skin of the immolated victim*." The *Globe*, the chief mouthpiece of the Democratic Party, expressed a position that would in the future become the possession of one or another of our political parties—that is, the hostility to corporate involvement in politics. The *Globe* editorial contained hostility to corporate involvement in politics, and sowed the seeds of legislation that would seek to restrict corporate participation in the electoral arena.

American political parties are a living testimony to what can be accomplished in a free society with volunteer involvement. Although theoretically the Communist Party of the Soviet Union is rooted in and controlled by the rank and file membership, in practice the party is controlled from the top. By comparison, the real home of political parties in the United States is not in the offices of the Democratic or Republican National Committees, nor, for that matter, in the White House. Rather, their home is in the states and, beyond that, in county and other local organizations where the rank and file contribute their time, energy, and money for the good of their party, the advancement of a cause, for personal and interest group advantage, and for personal gratification. By and large, this is also the nursery for candidates, nominees, and statesmen.

That all this is an extraconstitutional device of American politics, supported largely by lay volunteer activity, is a remarkable example of the capacities of a free people.

FOOTNOTES

[1] Harry V. Jaffa, *Equality and Liberty*, pp. 11-12
[2] Jaffa, pp. 18-25
[3] Jaffa, pp. 8-9
[4] Marvin Meyers, *The Jacksonian Persuasion*, pp. 15, 16

Chapter Four
Tocqueville: Democracy in America

In 1830 in the midst of a revolution in his native land, Alexis de Tocqueville, the precocious twenty-five year old son of a French aristocrat, sailed to America to make a study of prison reform. Although he completed his study of American prisons, his real discovery was the existence of a great democratic society unknown in its dimensions to even the most visionary of European thinkers. Above all, Tocqueville discovered the existence of an "equality of conditions"—that is, the existence of a society in which men actually lived on a plane of equality with one another.

In Europe, the vestiges of the *ancien regime* contested with the forces of republicanism for preeminence and power. There, the quest for equality was still an ideological battle ground. In America, by contrast, men lived peacefully according to a standard that seemed as native to the land as its flora and fauna.

Equality in America, according to Tocqueville, grew naturally from religious and political traditions that the first Americans carried with them from England. In addition, the vast extent of the country—the rich soil and agreeable climate, the absence of conditions that would support aristocratic institutions (for example, primogeniture), and the great distance of the Old World from the New—nurtured the process by which equality gradually spread into all the nooks and crannies of American society. The United States had its democracy, Tocqueville perceived, long before the Revolution of 1776—indeed, its seed is to be found in the culture of the first Englishmen to successfully colonize North America.

By comparison, the "lucky circumstances" that made for the gradual growth of American democracy were absent in the old societies of Europe. There, revolution succeeded revolution; the customs and institutions that made democracy in America an almost indigenous feature of the landscape would have to be artificially constructed if democracy was to be a wholesome and not a destructive force. Among the American institutions that most interested Tocqueville were civic and political associations.

The young Frenchman grasped the relationship between the tradition of voluntary associations and religious principle. If puritanism laid stress on liberty and individualism, it did so within the context of a community, freely formed of consenting members. Thus, individualism and associationalism developed side-by-side in America—the association served the individual needs of its members and the individual sacrificed immediate satisfaction of his needs for the common good of the membership. Above all, Tocqueville thought, it was only in such associations that mass democracy possessed a mediating vehicle between men, now more or less equal, and the power of government. Among other things, in a society where there are no artificial barriers of class or religion, voluntary associations are or should be "second nature." Men form and join them freely, and an associational tradition roots the very idea of "advocating by joining" into the habits, customs, and opinions of the people. Thus, the vehicle that mediates between the people and government is wholly consistent with the practice and spirit of democracy.

By comparison, in the middle ages, the aristocracy, monarchy, church, and guilds acted as checks upon one another, thwarting the accumulation of power in any one of these institutions; most men, however, did not qualify for membership, and those who did, followed a strict code imposed and maintained by hierarchical structures. Even after the French Revolution, the legacy of the *ancien regime* provided a culture in which voluntary associations were practically unknown and where the growth of centralized and bureaucratic government frustrated the possibility of their development. Where local associations or governments came into being, they were nearly always ordered by the central authority. This tradition was so strong on the continent that it was almost beyond the consciousness of Europeans even to conceive of "advocating by joining." Without the development of a tradition of voluntary associations, civil and political, democracy must inevitably give way to tyranny, Tocqueville believed.[1]

The chief function, then, of voluntary associations is preventing tyranny and securing liberty. Especially in ages of democracy, tyranny takes two forms: anarchy or mob rule, and plebiscitary democracy, often through the agency of a charismatic leader. Tocqueville describes these forms of tyranny under the rubric, "tyranny of the majority," and accounts for their origins. Where an equality of conditions is in the process of developing, the traditional links binding men together into communities—for example, the institutions of aristocracy, monarchy, church, and guilds—dissolve, leaving them only with opinion, individual or public, to guide their lives. The very nature of opinion, however, is that it fluctuates; under the rule of opinion, men are governed more by fashion, impulse, or immediate interest than by solid and enduring notions. The advantage of voluntary associations is that it checks both the dissolution or atomization of society, and the negative aspects of individualism by teaching men to seek the satisfaction of their interests in the company of others. It also teaches them to submit to the rules and customs of group government and the practices of cooperation and compromise—the civil behavior of democratic participation.

Voluntary associations are the nursery of democracy insofar as they teach individuals to submit to the will of the majority, majorities to observe the rights of individual members, and allow for individual experience and growth in assuming positions of leadership. This last lesson in particular prepares some persons to play a greater leadership role in other areas of society and government.

Tocqueville emphasized the role of private, voluntary associations in socializing individuals for participation in a democratic society. This, he thought, might check the potential anarchism of individualism that is always latent in a regime devoted to the actualization of human equality.

The other side of the coin, however, was equally important. The force of public opinion in mass democracy is almost unstoppable. Charismatic leaders, capturing the fancy of the many, can indulge demagoguery with impunity—especially where there are no intervening associations between the people and the government. Tocqueville saw this happen with his own eyes in his native land. Voluntary associations are the last resort of minority rights in societies that increasingly incline to plebiscitary democracy. Judged from this perspective, Tocqueville thought, the greater the number of mediating associations between the people and the government, the more hope for human liberty. As much as he cherished the idea of one humanity, he feared the notion of a uniformity of interests among men under one government.

Tocqueville was not lacking in concern or awareness of the potential danger freely-formed associations might hold for civil society. In many nations, after all, voluntary associations were a vehicle for revolutionary activity. Did not America have her Sons of Liberty? This, he believed, was a greater danger for Europeans than for Americans in 1830. And although he argued that freedom of political association was not the first among political rights, any government that tampered with it, he argued equally, comes precariously close to dismembering the right of people to govern themselves. "To save a man's life, I can understand cutting off his arm. But I don't want anyone to tell me that he will be as dexterous without it."[2] Indeed, Tocqueville understood the full danger and importance of voluntary associations—especially those he called "political associations."

Recently David Cohen, former President of Common Cause, spoke of "PAC democracy, with Congress representing the political action committees of America instead of its citizens."[3] Obviously Cohen was damning the role of political action committees in the last decade. By comparison, Tocqueville's language is no less to the point but his conclusion differs sharply. Tocqueville admits that political associations can be as "a separate nation within the nation and a government within the government." Moreover, he is keenly aware of their function and purpose: "... Americans every day (are) freely combining to make some political opinion triumph, to get some politician into the government, or to snatch power from another.... "[4] Furthermore, he is keenly perceptive about the attitude of government toward voluntary political committees:

> *In democratic countries political associations are, if one may put it so, the only powerful people who aspire to rule the state. Hence the governments of today look upon associations of this type much as medieval kings regarded the great vassals of the Crown; they feel a sort of instinctive abhorrence toward them and combat them whenever they meet.*[5]

Given these observations, Tocqueville still approved of the development of political associations as a support to free democratic societies. The overall lessons that democratic citizens learn as a result of their participation in political associations make them better, not worse, members of their nation. In addition, a nation within a nation and a government within a government is a necessary and important check on the possibility of tyranny. Moreover, the "industrial undertakings" of the Americans are their chief preoccupation, thus limiting the danger of political associations: "...(T)hese people who are so well occupied have no temptation to disturb the state or to upset the public calm by which they profit."[6] The involvement of Americans in civil and political associations, including what are today called "special interests," is critical to the success of democracy according to Tocqueville.

> *It is through political associations that Americans of every station, outlook, and age day by day acquire a general taste for association and get familiar with the way to use the same. Through them large numbers see, speak, listen and stimulate each other to carry out all sorts of undertakings in common. Then they carry these conceptions with them into the affairs of civil life and*

put them into a thousand uses.... In this way, by the enjoyment of a dangerous liberty, the Americans learn the art of rendering the dangers of freedom less formidable.[7]

Finally, Tocqueville cautions government to trespass on the right of association—especially political association—only with the greatest reserve. The direct and, particularly, the indirect consequences of such an act are subtle, long-range, and damaging in the extreme to the cause of liberty. Government must especially be cautious because it is its natural inclination, indeed, it is in its interest, to thwart the power of such groups. This hostility by government must be guarded against by an informed press, by an appropriate educational system that reaches both the electorate and actual or potential public officials, and by the efforts of voluntary associations themselves.

FOOTNOTES

[1] Tocqueville, Volume I, Part 2, chapters 5-7

[2] Tocqueville, Volume II, Part 2, chapter 7

[3] David Cohen, "Lets Free the Congress from PAC Domination," before the American Law Institute and the American Bar Association, April 11, 1980 in Arlington, Virginia

[4] Tocqueville, Volume II, Part 2, chapter 7

[5] *Ibid.*

[6] *Ibid.*

[7] *Ibid.*

Section III
The History of Voluntary Associations in America

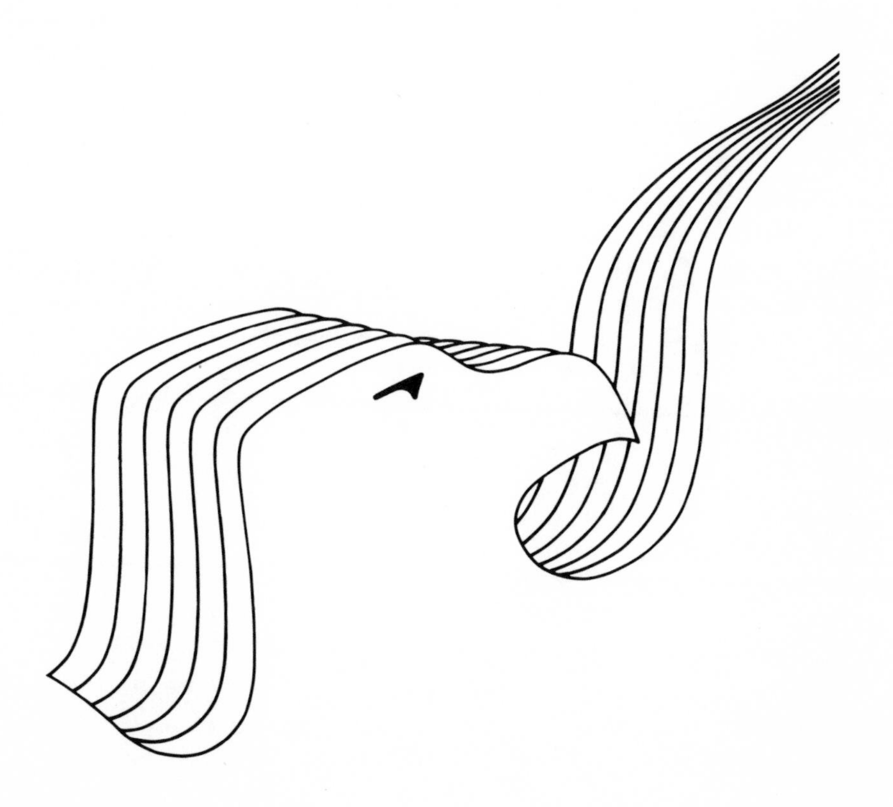

Chapter Five
The Colonial Experience

The origin of the tradition of voluntary associations in America is inseparable from the religious history of New England. When the first Puritans arrived in Massachusetts in 1630, they brought with them a number of interrelated concepts that were to affect profoundly the future course of American history. One was a sense of moral mission. Another was the notion of a covenant, or contract, linking each man to his church, his government, and his God, which could be abrogated whenever one of the contracting parties failed to uphold its part of the agreement. A third important concept brought to America by this community of "Saints" was the ideal of voluntary associations among individuals of like persuasion to establish communities for the purpose of a common end.

The night before this band of New World Israelites set foot into the American wilderness, their stately Governor, John Winthrop, proclaimed the purpose for which they commenced their exodus from England in a sermon delivered shipboard.

> *For the worke wee haue in hand, it is by a mutuall consent through a speciall overruleing providence, and a more then an ordinary approbation of the Churches of Christ to seeke out a place of Cohabitation and Consorteshipp vnder a due forme of Government both ciuill and ecclasiasticall.*[1]

Consent in addition to the blessing of God was to provide the foundation of both church and state, embedding the concept of voluntary associations into the consciousness and way of life of America's first permanent colonists. Their extraordinary mission was sustained by extraordinary piety and ambition—for what was at stake was nothing less than the founding of a New Jerusalem. Upon their success turned their salvation and their eternal reputation: "For wee must Consider that we shall be as a Citty vpon a Hill, the eies of all people are vppon vs."[2] The idea of voluntary associations, then, is partly the product of a religious ideal, carrying with it the deepest moral significance for mankind. No wonder that later generations of Americans believed that freely formed associations of men constituted the germ of democracy and, equally important, contained the power of human redemption.

The unique and distinguishing feature of New England Puritanism—the doctrine that separated it from the Church of England, the Presbyterian Puritanism of Britain and from the centrally-directed Calvinist churches of the Continent—was Congregationalism. The theology of American Puritanism held that a true church could be formed only by the voluntary association of believers. A person could not be born into a church, nor could he be compelled into church membership by governmental actions. A true church, as defined by the Massachusetts Bay Puritans, was a gathering of persons who came together out of their own free will; who were able to convince one another that they possessed saving grace; and who then voluntarily subscribed to a covenant with God and with each other, to honor and obey the divine laws and to perform whatever actions the Lord might require.

The doctrine of Congregationalism resulted in a system of church government in New England that was essentially associational. Towns grew up around churches, and were indeed inseparable from them. Each church and town represented a voluntary association of individuals, come together for the purpose of worshipping God, and enjoying something close to complete independence from all other churches and communities. Each congregation decided on its own membership, elected its own pastor and church officers, and financially supported its own activities by voluntary contributions. Each congregation, too, derived its authority directly from God, through its covenant with Him, and could subject itself to no other authority.

The New England Puritans believed that, ultimately, every nation and people existed only by virtue of its voluntary covenant with God, by which the people promised to obey the divine laws and God in turn bound Himself to treat the people with kindness. The Government and Church of England, however, through their various transgressions, including the attempt to suppress Puritan religious practices, had violated their part of the agreement, and thus invited divine wrath. And so the Puritans had come to America to establish a new covenant—a model nation in a new land. Here their mission was to create a society in which the Lord's will would be honored as closely as was humanly possible, and in which the sense of mission was ever-present. The voluntary association that was New England would serve as a "Citty vpon a hill," the ultimate fulfillment of the Reformation, and an example to all men of a truly saintly society.[3]

Three points should be noted about the influence of Puritanism on the origin and development of voluntary associations in America. First, the form and practice of congregational government, both church and state, has been the most important and enduring legacy left to the Americans by those early English voyagers to the New World. It has influenced nearly every denomination and has touched the lives of most men in two key areas of their corporate existence—church and state. In turn, the congregational model has been translated into habits and frame of mind by each succeeding generation of Americans, teaching them that the free association of individuals is the natural expression and vehicle for social, political, and economic activity.

Second, the congregational model became the seedbed for the development of democratic institutions and practices. Emphasizing that the only legitimate form of human association is composed of freely consenting individuals, congregational government brought into being institutions and practices that, if not fully resulting in a democratic creed in the seventeenth century, provided a cultural reception for the coming of democracy in the eighteenth. Above all, congregationalism was understood as opposing governmentally dictated structures—indeed was formulated in part as a response to the impositions of government on the freedom of men to define the mode of their own salvation.[4]

Third, the tradition of voluntary associations is born in America of a religious ideal. Indeed, voluntary associations have a sacred cast to them, thus making the freedom of association as cherished and hallowed as the freedom of religion. In fact, the freedom of religion decisively depends upon the full recognition of the freedom of men to associate voluntarily.

FOOTNOTES

[1] Perry Miller and Thomas H. Johnson, *The Puritans,* p. 197

[2] *Ibid.,* p. 199

[3] Perry Miller, *Errand Into the Wilderness,* Chapter I, pp. 1-15. See also Edmund S. Morgan, *The Puritan Dilemma,* Chapter VII: A Due Form of Government, pp. 84-100; and Daniel J. Boorstin, *The Americans,* pp. 3-31

[4] The authoratative defense of the congregational mode of church government was offered by John Wise in his "Vindication of the Government of New England Churches," *The Puritans,* pp. 257-269. See also, Sidney E. Mead, *The Lively Experiment,* Chapter II: From Coercion to Persuasion—Another Look at the Rise of Religious Liberty and the Emergence of Denominationalism, pp. 16-37; and *Errand Into the Wilderness,* pp. 2-23, 29-34

Chapter Six
Eighteenth Century America

Prior to the American Revolution, and during the first decade of the new republic, political associations sprang into being with the aim of influencing public opinion, elections, and government principally through programs of political education. Publishing broadsides and pamphlets, waging letter writing campaigns to newspapers—even founding newspapers—were common responses to an obnoxious policy, party, or public office holder. Indeed, prior to the twentieth century, the primary means of influencing elections was through newspaper advertisements. Expenditures for such programs often resembled what are today called "independent expenditures." The popular press, much more widespread and competitive than is the print media of our time, was also the most influential vehicle for reaching, persuading, and activating large numbers of voters. There is a long history of contributions by political associations to political campaigns through the popular press, the publication of broadsides and pamphlets, and the organization of parades and other public events.

Because public disclosure of campaign contributions is a relatively recent phenomenon, the history of contributions by private associations to candidates in eighteenth century America has received little attention by scholars of the period and there is little documentation for such practices. Moreover, election campaigns were brief, and office seekers tended to fund their candidacies out of pocket or from donations provided by friends, thus making campaign finance a subject seldom mentioned, let alone discussed as a public issue. In fact, the principal attention given to the subject turned around the scandalous practice of distributing money and "goods" to the electorate by candidates on or near election day. Since many, if not most, of the candidates for public office in colonial America were men of substance, this political practice was viewed as a failure of character, not as the responsibility of special interest associations or of a fault line in the political system. An attendant practice—"treating" the electorate to food and especially drink on election day—was also widely discussed, but was generally blamed on the individual candidate who usually provided the treats out of his own fortune. These problems of political corruption, which make the charges against the lawful contributions of today's political action committees look pale by comparison, were addressed by colonial legislatures as early as 1693.

Nevertheless, the available evidence suggests that civic and political associations devoted resources to election campaigns, and as the century progressed—especially after the adoption of the Constitution—this practice became even more varied and widespread. George Washington, for instance, in his election bid in 1757 to the Virginia House of Burgesses, "treated" his constituents on election day to liquor supplied by local merchants.[1] This form of "in-kind" contribution was a long standing, although often controversial, practice in colonial America. In 1791, groups opposed to Alexander Hamilton's economic policies organized to underwrite the cost of the *National Gazette*. It is believed that the *Gazette* sufficiently influenced public opinion to swing the Vice-Presidential electoral vote of such states as Virginia, North Carolina, and New York in the election of 1792. In response, pro-Hamiltonian groups subsidized the *Gazette of the United States*. During the 1790's, Jeffersonian newspapers railed against the "monied Associations" of Boston whose influence on the outcome of election campaigns blunted the interests of "mechanics and laborers"—followers of Jefferson—in key races.[2]

The American Revolution supplied additional impetus and a new direction to the development of voluntary associations. During the Stamp Act crisis of 1764-65, there appeared in every colony informal groups of men who called themselves "Sons of Liberty." These organizations were generally made up of merchants, lawyers, and other professionals, skilled artisans, and members of the propertied classes (the groups that had the most to lose from enforcement of the stamp tax), and eventually they formed a network that covered the colonies, with independent units in almost every town. The task of the Sons of Liberty was to coordinate and direct the protests and resistance against the Stamp Act, and they carried out their aim of defeating the tax by all means available to them. They also participated directly in political action, running the gamut from organizing boycotts, to harassing public officials, including efforts to unseat them, and raising mobs to threaten—or carry out—acts of violence against those colonists who either refused to cooperate or lent support to the royal government. These tactics led to the repeal of the Stamp Act in 1765; and although the Sons of Liberty ceased to function as political organizations after the repeal, the leading members throughout the colonies maintained contact with one another and continued their informal association through the communications network that had been established during the crisis.

During the crisis, the royal government sought to thwart the activities of the Sons of Liberty but were unsuccessful. The distance between England and America, in addition to the popularity of the cause in the colonies, frustrated the measures of the Crown. Indeed, the Crown was to be frustrated more than once by these freely constituted groups of "patriots." The presence of these vigilant and active voluntary associations made continual political cooperation in the colonies much more likely in the future and much more threatening to Britain's position and ambitions in America.

The antecedents of today's political action committee can be traced to the Sons of Liberty. The latter developed a program of political education, and devoted energy, time, and money to unseating public officials on grounds of principle and interest. And although some of their motives, techniques, and activities should not receive approbation, the cause of the Sons of Liberty was popular and was sustained by the idea that it is unjust to tax a people against their will. Rallying around an economic injustice, the American colonists understood well—perhaps better than many Americans today—the relationship of economic liberty and the powers of government. Moreover, they experienced the effort of government to limit and sequester their activities—an effort that failed—although one that also left an indelible imprint on their memories. Finally, they learned about the techniques and the advantages of voluntary political action—and established the roots of a tradition that has influenced and characterized the American political experience.

Many more voluntary associations sprang up in the colonies during the early 1770's, as King and Parliament sought to reassert their authority. Responding to a British plan for paying colonial judges and royal governors out of customs revenues—rather than having their pay voted by the elected colonial assembly—the rabble-rousing Sam Adams organized the Boston Committee of Correspondence in 1772. Within a few months, there were some eighty such committees in Massachusetts alone, and similar organizations had come into existence in every colony. In an effort to bring about concerted colonial action in the continuing confrontation with Great Britain, the Committees of Correspondence circulated letters, petitions, and propaganda from one end of British North America to the other. These voluntary associations were, in effect, vital cogs in the revolutionary machine; and with their overriding goal of promoting intercolonial solidarity, they were part of an initial effort to join the colonies in some kind of political union.

Nor should one neglect the important role of voluntary associations in the Revolutionary War itself. The colonial militia that first laid siege to the city of Boston, and that later provided the bulk of the manpower for the American war effort, was in a sense a volunteer military organization. Though poorly trained, lacking in discipline, and supplied only with such weapons as the men themselves could provide, the militia managed to harass British forces constantly; to provide essential reinforcements to state and Continental regiments of the line; to nullify most British efforts at reimposing royal authority; and, finally, to convince London that it could not hope to win a decisive victory in a war against a people in arms. These were considerable accomplishments for a military force that was, throughout the war, looked upon with some contempt by the regular troops of both sides.

FOOTNOTES

[1] George Thayer, *Who Shakes the Money Tree?: American Campaign Financing Practices from 1789 to the Present,* 1973, p. 25. Also see, Douglas Southall Freeman, *George Washington,* Vol. II, 1948, p. 318. "Treating" was to come to an end shortly as a political practice of Washington—in Freeman, Vol. III, pp. 141-142

[2] Thayer, p. 26

Chapter Seven
Jacksonian America

The exuberant spirit of Jacksonian America was manifested in the widespread diffusion of associational activities, both secular and religious. The new religious groups were, for the most part, evangelical in origin, and sprang from the great outburst of religious revivalism that swept the country in the period between the 1820's and the 1840's. This spiritual awakening, which was particularly evident on the Northwest frontier and in that area of western New York known as the "Burned-Over District"—an area largely settled by transplanted New Englanders who brought with them the spirit of revival that first swept the country during the Great Awakening of 1740-1760—also gave rise to a number of voluntary associations aimed at remedying specific social evils. Furthermore, during this period a variety of communal social experiments were begun which were intended to inspire other men with a faith in the ultimate perfectibility of human social institutions.

The religious revival of the 1820's through the 1840's generated a new wave of enthusiasm in religion and the founding of additional sects and churches to add to the already bulging catalogue of American faiths. In a regime devoted to the principle of religious freedom, religion prospered through an ever increasing multiplicity of sects. Throughout this period, religious and political themes intermixed—indeed, it was often difficult to tell where religion left off and politics began. In part, this was due to the fact that religion—more specifically, biblical religion—supplied the cultural matrix of American society. The Mormons, as did the Puritan settlers before them, saw themselves as "new Israelites," founding not only a communion but also a community. As part of their religious practice they sought to establish "a way of life," regulating faith as well as ethical behavior, and providing for a governing authority that could maintain both. These associations were made possible by a country that was characterized by a large extent of territory and a commitment to the freedoms of association and religion.

If the Mormons, the Shakers, the Millerites, and many others sought to establish "a way of life," other denominations, often associated with mainline Protestant churches, sought to address specific social evils. In the 1840's, for example, reform groups all over the Northeast came together to advocate more humane treatment of criminals and of persons confined to mental institutions. Concern for criminals, paupers, and the insane was also closely related to another goal of the antebellum reform movement: temperance. It was commonly believed that excessive drinking was a basic cause of the condition of these unfortunates, as well as of poverty in general. Temperance groups, therefore, believed that they could not only redeem the individual sinner, but could advance as well the entire course of society. Numerous local temperance societies were formed in the early 1820's, and this led, in 1826, to the creation of a national organization, the American Society for the Promotion of Temperance. Under the prodding of the various temperance groups, by the mid-1850's a dozen states had passed prohibition laws.[1]

Peace societies and women's rights groups also proliferated in the years prior to the Civil War. In 1828, the country's many local peace groups came together to form the American Peace Society, the primary goal of which was the establishment of a Congress of Nations to interpret international law, and of a Court of Nations to apply that law. The women's groups won a number of significant victories under the leadership of such fiery feminists as Elizabeth Cady Stanton, Frances Wright, and Lucretia Mott. After the first national convention of the women's rights movement, at Seneca Falls, New York, in 1848, women began to secure admission to institutions of higher learning and to such professions as literature, medicine, and education.

By the beginning of the 1850s, however, all of these many reform associations were beginning to be overshadowed in America by the cause of abolitionism. Eventually, most of the nation's leading reformers came to the conclusion that human slavery was the single social evil blocking the path to America's moral regeneration; only a great moral crusade, they believed, could end this mortal offense against the laws of God, and guarantee the survival of American liberty. Loosely organized under the aegis of the American Antislavery Society (founded in 1833), the numerous state and local abolitionist groups throughout the North and West mounted a campaign to educate the public on the evils of slavery, and to promote political action that would first contain, and then destroy, the South's "peculiar institution."

The principal plank of the abolitionist platform was to work against all those who directly or indirectly supported slavery. They refused to cooperate with either the Whig or Democratic parties, and their opposition to anyone tainted by their compromise with the slave holding states translated into efforts to defeat officials and other candidates for public office whose opinions and actions they found objectionable. Although the principal expression of this sentiment took the form of newspaper advertisements endorsing or opposing particular candidates, it also generated in limited amounts direct contributions to office seekers. The abolitionist movement demonstrates that single-issue politics is not a phenomenon of the 1970s, but is deeply rooted in American political history.

Various associations were divided on the question of slavery and the preservation of the Union throughout the period of this contest. For instance, in New York City, merchant associations, fearing the dislocation to commerce in the event of a conflict between North and South, "devoted much of their time and a good deal of their private funds for more than a decade to the task of defeating politicians whom they regarded as enemies of the union." Associations of merchants, however, also supported the cause of abolition with funds to political candidates—joining the Republican Party out of the belief that Southern threats of secession could only disrupt the economic and political life of the nation on a continuing basis.

These voluntary associations, committed to the eradication of social evil, mixed religion, morality, and politics in a way that is uniquely American. They also collected contributions, generated programs of public education, and sought to elect friendly public officials and unseat "sinners." This, too, is uniquely American. Once again we see the outline of today's political action committee in what was by the 1820's already an ongoing part of an American political tradition. Surely the zeal of those groups would have led them to condemn as the devil's own work any attempt by government to limit or regulate their activities.

Also growing out of the religious enthusiasm and social activism of the Jacksonian period were the various experiments in utopian socialism that suddenly abounded in America. These socialistic communities, built by the naive but determined efforts of like-minded people, were meant to serve as the models for a new and better social order. To some extent, they did represent the desire of their founders to escape from the unpleasantness and pressures of the real world outside. To a much greater extent, however, these experiments in communal living served to demonstrate the zeal for human reform that was rampant in the America of the Jacksonian period. In their ideal little societies, the communitarians believed that people of good will and like mind might find solutions to the great problems of the day; and their utopian experiments might then stand forth as examples to all mankind of how fraternal cooperation could solve many of the world's troubles.

Brightest and happiest of the utopian communities was Brook Farm in Massachusetts, a socialistic creation of the leading New England Transcendentalists. Much longer-lived, and far more controversial, was the Oneida community of John Humphrey Noyes, whose followers sought to turn such innovations as free love and socialized manufacturing plants into a recipe for prosperity, happiness, and a complete release from earthly sin.

Other utopian experiments in America during these years included Robert Owen's New Harmony, Indiana. Owen was a well-known Scottish socialist who had earlier established model villages for the workers at his Lanark, Scotland, textile mills, which were objects of study by manufacturers and social reformers alike. At New Harmony, where he had purchased the land from a disillusioned group of Shakers, Owen undertook to rehabilitate 2,400 working-class people ("the dregs of the dregs of society") by a regime of work, rest, play, study, and meditation. In promoting his scheme and enlisting the 2,400 souls, Owen made it sound as though his colony would usher in the millenium; his experiment, however, failed within two years—a victim of human nature.

Owen's failure, however, did not prevent other idealists from setting up utopian experiments. Frances Wright set up a colony at Neshoba, Tennessee, where a group of slaves were to live together and earn their freedom with their labor in five years. Neshoba, unfortunately, did not last five years. The Jacksonian period was also the great time of popularity in America for the doctrine of association developed by the French socialist, Francois Charles Fourier. Altogether more than forty such Fourierist settlements (called "phalanxes") were set up in various parts of America in the 1830's and 1840's. The residents of each phalanx spent the days working in the community's fields or shops, and the evenings in artistic work, intellectual endeavors, or meditation. These associations, too, were short-lived. But, before their failure, they testified anew to the American faith in voluntary association as a means of accomplishing desired social ends, and of uniting individuals into groups and communities that could serve as inspirational examples to the rest of the world.[2]

They also demonstrated that the freedom that allows for the proliferation of voluntary associations belongs neither to the "right" nor the "left" of the social, political, and economic spectrum. Americans of all religious, moral, and political persuasions have experimented with voluntary associations, sought to advance their views and have others adopt them, and exercised influence for the sake of a principle or an interest to which their membership subscribed. It may well have been thought by the Mormons or the socialist experimenters of Jacksonian America that the effort to curb the activities of unpopular associations might just lead to similar actions later against other groups falling into public disfavor.

Among the general conclusions that may be drawn about the many voluntary associations of antebellum America, it may be said that most were inspired by the evangelical spirit of the times; that they were dedicated to moral ends; that they were full of faith in the inevitability of progress and the perfectibility of man and of human institutions; and that they believed both in the worth of the individual, and in the ability of individuals, united in a common cause, to change the face of society and to lead America toward the fulfillment of its moral and political mission. In these years of America's youth, the great profusion of voluntary associations reflected the naive and buoyant optimism of a deeply religious and profoundly idealistic nation.

FOOTNOTES

[1] Cherrington, Ernest Hurst, *The Evolution of Prohibition in the United States of America,* 1969; especially chapters IV and V

[2] For a discussion of these and other communal experiments in America, see Albert Fried, *Socialism in America,* 1970

Chapter Eight
America Comes of Age

In the period of American history referred to as the "Gilded Age" (between the end of the Civil War and the beginning of the twentieth century), industrialization changed the face of the United States. At the time of Appomattox, the country was overwhelmingly rural and agricultural; by 1900, it was an industrial and urban giant, in a state of permanent and accelerating change.

The last three decades of the nineteenth century were often difficult and confusing for many Americans, yet they held more opportunities and hope for progress than in any other time in American history. Businessmen, workers, farmers, and members of the emerging middle class often found they could not cope individually with the rapid pace of progress and the economic and social changes that inevitably resulted. They soon discovered, however, that as organized groups—as voluntary associations of individuals seeking common ends—they could wield considerable power. Increasingly, then, in the late nineteenth century, individual efforts gave way to common action. In the new industrial society, more decisions were being made by well-organized groups.

Among the most successful and lasting of these groups were those formed by American businessmen. The corporation itself was a form of voluntary association which, by combining the resources of many people in a joint endeavor, differed significantly from individual enterprise. More significant still were the various forms of business organization adopted by American industrialists in the late nineteenth century to gain greater control over markets and resources. The first business pools—informal agreements among producers of similar products—came into being in the 1870's. Later, the Standard Oil Company pioneered a tighter and more effective form of business cooperation—the trust. And after 1890, the holding company became a popular method for controlling a large number of firms. This was also the first great age of business mergers in America; in the wake of the Panic of 1893, the number of such combinations rose from 12 to 305, and by 1904 these firms controlled almost two-fifths of the manufacturing capital in the United States.

Businessmen also organized nationally in such bodies as the National Board of Trade, the National Business League, and the National Association of Manufacturers. In the wake of the developing muscle of state and federal government over the business community, these groups were intended to educate the public and influence the types of state and national legislation that might affect business enterprise. At the local level this period saw an enormous expansion in the number of community trade associations and chambers of commerce in the United States.

As a response to the new role and strength of American business, labor unions gradually and painfully rose to prominence in the final decades of the nineteenth century. Some attempts to unionize, such as the actions of the Molly Maguires in the northeastern coal fields in the 1870's, and the poorly conceived efforts of the Knights of Labor in the 1880's, were far from successful.

For instance, the Noble Order of the Knights of Labor proved itself an association that was doomed by uncertainty over its goals and how they could be won. First established in 1869 by the Philadelphia garment workers, the Knights did not expand into a national organization until 1878, when their convention at Reading, Pennsylvania declared that henceforth they would welcome any person "who at any time worked for wages."[1] After several successful strikes in 1884-85 against a number of major railroads, the Knights of Labor grew to embrace some 700,000 workers. But within five years, the organization was moribund and without a significant labor following. It had been destroyed by the diverse interests of its membership; the uncertainty of its leadership (even after the successful strike action of 1884-85, Terrence V. Powderley remained opposed to the idea of strikes); its conflict with other, more militant labor groups; its disdainful neglect of unskilled workers; and its failure to win a number of crucially important strikes in the late 1880's.

Other national labor unions, however, organized by specific trade, made significant gains in the late nineteenth century. In 1886, the American Federation of Labor was overhauled under the leadership of Samuel Gompers, formerly of the Cigarmakers' Union. Under Gompers, the AF of L commenced its effort to coordinate the national unions in support of legalized strikes, boycotts, and picketing, and the shorter hours, higher pay, and greater fringe benefits that were the major goals of most union members. By 1904, the AF of L counted a membership in excess of 1.6 million workers, and the unions had established themselves as a permanent part of the American economy.

Pressed to action by the glut of farm products that depressed prices throughout the late nineteenth century, American farmers also formed numerous voluntary action groups in the post-Civil War period. For a time the Patrons of Husbandry were the favorite farm order, and it was argued that the major goal of such groups should be to improve rural social life and end the farmers' isolated and drab existence. The social gatherings, however, soon grew into occasions for attacks on the malpractices of the railroads, and out of this agitation arose the Granger movement of the 1870s. The movement was short-lived, but it did succeed in establishing the right of the states to regulate in some degree the business of common carriers. In the 1880s, locally chartered Farmers' Alliances were organized throughout the Old Northwest and the New South, and these were eventually united into regional associations of considerable political influence. There were almost a thousand local Alliances in the Midwest by 1881, and by 1890 the Southern Alliance had between 1 and 3 million members. At the state and regional level, the Northern and Southern Alliances were dedicated to fighting eastern "monopolists" and exercising political influence; at the local level, the Alliance organizations sponsored social activities, promoted agricultural education, set up local cooperatives for purchasing machinery and marketing crops, and distributed literature on scientific farming and on the social and political questions of the day.[2]

By 1890, Alliance political activities were aimed primarily at securing regulation of the railroads, the breakup of trusts, controls on banks, low interest rates, cheap money, and a number of mechanisms to further the cause of populist democracy. By 1890, also, there was a strong demand within the Alliances, especially in the Midwest, for an independent farmers' political party. The result, of course, was the birth of the People's (or Populist) Party in 1892, and its eventual fusion with free-silver Democrats in 1896. After the defeat of Bryan in 1896, and the return of farm prosperity in the first decade of the twentieth century, the voluntary associations of farmers lost much of their political importance.

Finally, there were the numerous organizations established in the late nineteenth century by the members of America's increasingly influential professional middle class. The new industrial economy had need for a large number of well-educated and highly trained professionals, and the nation's maturing educational system was readily turning them out in these years. And as the numbers grew of persons with professional aspirations in such fields as medicine, law, economics, administration, social work, and the arts—and as the specialists in business, labor, and agriculture awakened to their distinctiveness—it was almost inevitable that new voluntary associations would spring up to unite the new professionals. Hence, more and more middle class persons of like interests joined together to provide themselves with intellectual stimulus, social interaction, and, in some cases, political clout.

Without attempting to provide any sort of systematic classification of the new professional groups, or even to list more than a tiny number of them, it may be pointed out that the years about the end of the nineteenth century and the beginning of the twentieth saw the creation of: the National Education Association; the Modern Language Association; the American Bar Association; the American Library Association; the Archaeological Institute of America; the American Mathematical Society; the American Physical Society; the American Economics Association; the American Psychological Association; the American Historical Association; the American Sociological Society; the American Political Science Association; and the American Conference of Social Work.

Although the development of voluntary associations among businessmen, workers, farmers, and professional people lacked some of the moral fervor and religious inspiration of many earlier associations, the form and function of these post-Civil War groups corresponded in many important respects to their predecessors. After all, by now Americans had come to believe—"in their bones"—that the only legitimate and successful form of political activity was through voluntary associations. In the post-Civil War period groups of persons freely organized associations for mutual interest and shared principle at an ever increasing rate. Their concerns were economic, social, and professional—and all desired and worked towards increasing political influence for their point of view. The means by which people acted on their own behalf had become so firmly established by this period that Americans could not think of matters of interest or principle without forming a committee "to do something about it."

FOOTNOTES

[1] Powderly, T. V., *Thirty Years of Labor, 1859 to 1889; In Which the History of the Attempts to form Organizations of Workingmen for the Discussion of Political, Social and Economic Questions is Traced.* (Philadelphia, 1890), p. 131. At Reading, the Knights adopted their Constitution. In their Preamble, they stated a number of political goals. According to one commentator: "In accepting the Preamble of the Industrial Brotherhood, the consention fully realized that for the most part the reforms which were asked for in that Preamble must one day come through political agitation and action."

[2] Buck, Solon Justus, *The Granger Movement: A Study of Agricultural Organization and its Political, Economic and Social Manifestations,* 1870-1880 (Cambridge: Harvard University Press, 1913). The chapter entitled "Conclusion," provides an overall summary of the origin and relationship of the various agricultural associations that sought to wield political power during the latter third of the century.

Chapter Nine
The Progressive Era

It was in the Progressive era preceding American entry into the European War that the middle class really began to organize for political action. Indeed, the phenomenon known as Progressivism won its start in the coalescing of middle class reform groups, mainly in the great cities of the Northeast and the Middle West, around the turn of the century. Spurred to action by the numerous ills besetting or perceived to beset American urban life in this period, groups of small businessmen, intellectuals, union officials, public administrators, social workers, doctors, lawyers, teachers, and clergymen began to come together in Urban Reform Leagues, City Clubs, Municipal Ownership Leagues, and Direct Legislation Leagues. By 1905, such nonpartisan, "good government" action groups dotted the land, and were busily seeking solutions to the urban problems of vice, crime, corruption, slum housing, child labor, inadequate lighting, untreated sewage, and poor public transportation. Some of the Progressive organizations provided sponsorship for settlement houses in the midst of slum neighborhoods (the most famous, of course, was Jane Adams' Hull House in Chicago). Others lobbied Chambers of Commerce to finance pilot projects aimed at improving the lot of slum children.

In many cities, Municipal Voter Leagues were established as small, autonomous political units, which could overcome local machine politics by nominating, electing, and controlling their own people in city government. To provide aid to newcomers from Europe who were pouring into urban areas, a group of Northeastern businessmen in 1908 formed the North American Civic League for Immigrants. Other reformist coalitions pushed for more nurseries and kindergartens for the children of working class mothers; for better schools; for recreational facilities and social clubs in urban neighborhoods; for improved health standards; for better treatment of criminals; and for a reorganization of municipal government. The American Civic Association promoted the creation of city parks and sports programs for the benefit of urban youngsters.

In New York City, a group known as the "Committee of Fifteen" carried out a year-long investigation of tenement housing in 1900; a year later, many of the Committee's recommendations were embodied in a new state law that set minimum standards for lighting, sanitation, ventilation, and fire protection. In Cincinnati a few years later, a band of urban Progressives volunteered for an effort to turn a rundown industrial subdivision of the city into a model of a professionally serviced community. The successes and failures of all these groups were well known to municipal reformers all across the country, since the National Municipal League had been established to serve as a nationwide clearinghouse for information on such matters.[1]

Other Progressive reform organizations in these years united consumers, Social Gospelers, advocates of labor legislation, and representatives of rural America. One of the most active national associations was the General Federation of Women's Clubs, whose one million members devoted enormous amounts of time and energy to social issues. Another women's organization, the National Consumers' League, fought with a great deal of success to force employers to provide better working conditions in industrial plants. Reinforcing these efforts was the work of the American Association for Labor Legislation, whose volunteer lawyers specialized in drawing up model statutes for consideration by state legislatures.

The problem of child labor was another major issue raised by Progressives. In 1914, a group of union officials, social workers, lawyers, and professional people, confederated under the title of the National Child Labor Committee, drew up the first Congressional bill to deal seriously with the problem. Working in support of this group were such new nationwide organizations as the National Federation of Settlements (formed by social workers in 1911), the Federal Council of Churches (formed by reformist Protestant clergymen in 1900), and the National Conference of Catholic Charities (founded in 1910).

In the Middle West, meanwhile, Progressive legislation was supported in state capitals by coalitions of merchants, commercial farmers, lawyers, bankers, promoters, and newspaper editors. Eventually the region's farmers came together in such activist associations as the Non-Partisan League, the National Farmers' Union, and the American Society of Equity—all of which were dedicated to a dynamic program of governmental intervention to promote agricultural interests.

As the national reform movement went forward under the leadership of such Progressive politicians as Theodore Roosevelt and Woodrow Wilson, many other voluntary associations were organized to further social legislation and humanitarian endeavors. The National Housing Association sought federal standards for the housing industry; the National Pure Food and Drug Congress, and the Committee of One Hundred on National Health, worked for improvements in the food Americans consumed. The National Conference of Charities and Corrections fought for a federal minimum wage, for workmen's compensation laws, and for widows' and orphans' pensions. Increased regulation of railroads was the goal of the National Industrial Traffic League. Innumerable women's suffrage groups lobbied for enactment of a Constitutional amendment granting them the right to vote, while the National Association for the Advancement of Colored People demanded political, economic, and social equality for Negroes.

Nearly always, it may be said, the Progressives marched in groups—in voluntary associations that aimed at pinpointing problems, advertising their existence, and offering the ways and means of curing them. The Progressive era saw the beginnings of the "good government" movement, and what is today called "public interest" groups. Reacting to real and perceived wrongs in American society, they sought solutions to problems through democratizing and depoliticizing the political process. This was, perhaps, a natural attitude for an emerging middle class who represented neither labor nor capital in the classic sense.

For instance, as to the charge that "big" business exercised undue influence over state legislatures adverse to the interests of the consumer and the laborer, good government groups advocated the initiative, the referendum, and the direct election of United States Senators. Democratizing the political system, it was believed, would take the "politics out of politics," thus providing a solution to corrupt political practices. Whatever the merits of this philosophy—for surely direct popular participation in the political system has not taken the "politics out of politics"—the cause was popular and successful. Once again we see the results of voluntary associations. For in almost all cases, the reform of the political system was begun initially by small groups of individuals, self-selecting and freely constituted, sharing common concerns, and seeking broader public acceptance through programs of political education, and contributions of time, energy, expertise, and money to candidates for public office.

During this period of American history perhaps the two most successful political movements were generated by associations—the Anti-Saloon League, and the National American Women's Suffrage Association in combination with the Congressional Union. Both the prohibitionists and the suffragettes worked at the state and national levels, seeking referenda and constitutional amendments for their special causes. Moreover, both were generated and sustained by associations possessing strong, hierarchical structures—especially the Anti-Saloon League—and effective delivery systems for political education. Their ability to inform their constituents about friendly and unfriendly office holders is a model of political and organizational efficiency. Indeed, all three associations devoted the resources of their memberships—in the millions of dollars—to help pass legislation at the state and national levels and to contribute money to helpful candidates and to defeat those legislators they found to be obnoxious.[2] Finally, these associations—turning into movements, if not crusades—were successful in their immediate goals. Once again we see examples of the role and impact of single issue associations on the history of American politics. In many respects they represent the model of modern political action associations in their organization, in their programs of political education, in their fund raising ability, and in their effectiveness. They are also models in other respects—especially when compared with contemporary single issue associations and movements.

FOOTNOTES

[1] For a comprehensive account of the subject see Frank Mann Stewart, *A Half Century of Municipal Reform; The History of the National Municipal League,* 1950. For a listing of the League's publications see Alva W. Stewart, *The National Municipal League: A Bibliographical Survey,* 1978.

[2] The history of the Anti-Saloon League is best told in Peter H. Odegard's *Pressure Politics: The Story of the Anti-Saloon League,* 1966. This volume is "must" reading for anyone who wants to better understand the relationship of association organizations and political influence.

Chapter Ten
The 1920's

Despite their great vitality in the years prior to 1917, many of the Progressive organizations failed to persist into the 1920's. The heart went out of reformism during America's brief but bloody experience with the war in Europe, and in the decade that followed, voluntary associations of a different sort came to the fore, while older activist groups either disappeared altogether or lost much of their former vigor. The only organization that could pretend to speak for a large body of workers in the post-war period, the American Federation of Labor, suffered serious reverses during the Twenties; a number of important judicial decisions went against the unions, and public opinion was hostile to anything that smelled of "radicalism." Between 1920 and 1923, the AF of L lost 25 percent of its membership, and by 1930 its members had been reduced to fewer than four million of the country's twenty-four million blue-collar workers.[1]

Farm organizations, too, fared poorly in the Twenties. The most active and influential voluntary association of farmers, the Farm Bureau Federation, mainly represented only the most successful farmers of the upper Middle West. The farm cooperative movement was also pretty much confined to this region, while the more distressed farmers of the South and Great Plains were without organizations that could have given them political influence. Among the segments of the population that proved most active in forming voluntary associations were racial, ethnic, and religious minorities. In part, this activity was inspired by old loyalties that the war years had awakened in "hyphenated

Americans," and by the emergence of new independent states like Poland, Hungary, Latvia, Lithuania, Estonia, Finland, and Yugoslavia. The chauvinism of American minorities was a reaction to the anti-foreign temperment that gripped many Americans, and that demanded the "Americanization" of the new immigrants. Whatever the cause, the decade saw the emergence of fraternal organizations representing Latvians, Serbs, Croats, Letts, Slovaks, and others.

By 1925, the Sons of Italy counted 125,000 members in 887 lodges; the National Polish Alliance had 130,000 members in 1,700 lodges;[2] even the Japanese Association of America claimed a membership in the thousands. The nation's Catholics, meanwhile, had established the National Catholic Welfare Conference to coordinate creation of such groups as the Catholic Boy Scouts and the Catholic Total Abstinence Union. And in activities intended to boost the pride of America's most consistently oppressed minority, Marcus Garvey organized the "Back to Africa" movement (which had five million dues-paying believers at its height), and W.E.B. Dubois of the NAACP arranged for "Pan African Congresses" to harmonize the ideas and actions of black Americans.

The startling growth of the Ku Klux Klan during the decade gave some impetus to the movement for association among minority groups. Reorganized on Stone Mountain, Georgia, in November, 1915, the Klan during the next ten years moved out of the Deep South and established itself as the chief organ of anti-foreign and anti-Catholic hostility. In 1920, there were only 5,000 klansmen; by 1925, there were nine million, and in some states they were powerful enough to nominate and elect their own statewide political candidates. For a few years, the KKK was the favored association of many American small towns.[3]

For their influence on American society, however, the most powerful voluntary groups of the 1920's were the national trade associations. With the encouragement of the Republican administrations in Washington—and especially of Commerce Secretary Herbert Hoover—thousands of American businessmen organized into associations designed to standardize products, pool information and resources, purchase raw materials, and enforce industry codes. Between 1920 and the end of the Hoover presidency, the number of trade associations in the United States increased from a handful to more than 2,000.[4]

FOOTNOTES

[1] U.S. Department of Commerce, Bureau of the Census, *Historical Statistics of the United States*, "Series D 940-945, Labor Union Membership, by Affiliation: 1897 to 1934; " "Series D 182-232, Major Occupation Group of the Experienced Civilian Labor Force, by Sex: 1900 to 1970."

[2] Studies of these groups include: Antonio Mansano, *Sons of Italy*, 1971; and the National Fraternal Congress of America, *Statistics for Fraternal Societies*, 39th edition

[3] *Washington Post*, November 2, 1930, p. 14

[4] See Joseph F. Bradley *The Role of Trade Associations and Professional Business Societies*, pp. 17-45, for a brief history of the development and expansion of the trade association phenomenon.

Chapter Eleven
The New Deal

The Democratic administration of Franklin Roosevelt did not take any immediate action against the trade associations. On the contrary, in the national planning phase of Roosevelt's New Deal, the trade associations served an extremely important function. Under the terms of the National Industrial Recovery Act—the legislative centerpiece of the First New Deal—the trade associations were delegated power to draw up the industrial codes of conduct for their respective industries; more important, trade association officials, who almost invariably represented the largest corporations participating in each industry, were picked to staff most of the code authorities that were responsible for administering and enforcing the NRA codes. By resting such great power and authority in the trade associations, and then furthering their activities by temporarily suspending the antitrust laws, the early Roosevelt administration gave impetus to monopolistic tendencies in the American economy. It also established a precedent by placing voluntary associations under the wing of government. In the name of cooperation, it subjected business oriented voluntary associations to regulation and control.[1]

The Agricultural Adjustment Act—another piece of Roosevelt legislation that was central to his program of national planning until it was declared unconstitutional in 1935—also depended heavily for its administration on the activities of voluntary associations. In this case, however, the associations in question were organized by large-scale farmers, in order to administer AAA controls on the local planting and harvesting of crops. Unfortunately, empowering such local groups to decide what crops should be curtailed, and in what quantities, again placed enormous power in the hands of the largest producers, who nearly always dominated local and county agricultural associations. There were no real safeguards for the smaller and more weakly organized producers, and hence small farmers benefited little from the AAA; many of the poorest tenant farmers and sharecroppers in the South and Southwest, in fact, ended up being expelled from their lands as a result of AAA planning.[2]

Some of the small farmers, however, organized their own voluntary associations to combat such eventualities, and to struggle against the low prices and threats of foreclosure that plagued American agriculturists during most of the Depression years. In July of 1934, for example, a little band of white and black tenant farmers in Arkansas put together the Southern Tenant Farmers' Union, to resist the expulsion of tenants by the large landowners who controlled the local AAA administration. Despite a campaign of terror and intimidation aimed at Union members by those who feared both the alleged radicalism of the group and its implications of racial equality, by 1937 the Tenant Farmers' Union had attracted 35,000 members in Arkansas and Oklahoma. In that year, it affiliated with the Council of Industrial Organizations, and thereafter maintained a lively lobby in the national capital.

Meanwhile, in the Midwest, radical farm sentiment found expression in the so-called Farm Holiday Association, organized in 1932 to try to persuade farmers that they ought to withhold their products from the market until prices rose to meet the cost of production. In the spring of 1933, striking members of this group held a number of Midwestern cities under virtual siege, threatening to organize a nationwide strike while they blocked roads to prevent agricultural products from reaching urban consumers. Midwestern farmers also formed vigilante committees to frighten away potential buyers from foreclosure sales, or to buy back foreclosed properties at nominal sums and then return them to their former owners.

American labor made great strides in membership in the Great Depression largely through increased reliance on voluntary associations. In 1937, John L. Lewis led the break of the Council of Industrial Organizations from the American Federation of Labor, and during the next few months the CIO more than doubled its membership (from 1.8 million to 3.7 million) through massive efforts to establish vertical unions within some of the nation's largest industries. Lewis also played a key role in the creation of big labor's so-called Non-Partisan League, which rallied support for many pieces of New Deal legislation, and raised large amounts of money for Roosevelt's re-election campaigns.[3] From the Non-Partisan League, the contemporary political action committee was born.

Labor's success in the field of politics and the general thrust of the New Deal further alarmed American conservatives, who had busied themselves since the beginning of Roosevelt's presidency with the organizing of voluntary associations to resist his "dictatorial" manner and "socialistic" programs. Among such groups were the American Liberty League and the National Committee to Uphold Constitutional Government. Neither organization enjoyed much success in rallying popular opposition to the New Deal.

For a short time, however, a number of other associations, each of them led by a persuasive individual who promised salvation from the miseries of the Depression, seemed to present serious threats to the cohesiveness of the Roosevelt coalition. In California, the EPIC (End Poverty in California) movement, led by the muckraking novelist Upton Sinclair, attracted thousands of followers with a program that promised statewide prosperity through the creation of rural communes and the levying of huge taxes on the wealthy; Sinclair came close to being elected governor of the state before his movement broke up in 1934. On the national level, the New Deal was also challenged by such figures as Dr. Francis E. Townsend, of Long Beach, and the Reverend Charles E. Coughlin, a Roman Catholic priest from the suburbs of Detroit. So popular was the so-called Townsend Plan, which promised to pay $200 a month out of the federal treasury to every unemployed American over the age of 60, that by 1935 there were more than 1,200 Townsend Clubs, or Old Age Revolving Pension Clubs, in the United States. Among other things, the Townsend program contributed to the speedy approval by Congress of the Social Security Act in 1935. As for Father Coughlin, his National Union for Social Justice, organized in 1934 to lobby for the nationalization of banks, utilities, and natural resources, had several hundred thousand members by the end of 1935. The National Union's decline did not come until the end of the decade, when Coughlin changed the name of the organization to the Christian Front, and began openly to proclaim his anti-Semitic and pro-Nazi sentiments.[4]

Indeed, the troubled international climate of the 1930's was reflected in the character of many American voluntary associations. In addition to Coughlin's Christian Front, there existed on the political right such groups as the Committee of One Million in Detroit—a Negrophobic, anti-Communist, and Jew-baiting group—and the Silvershirt Legion, a nationwide fascist organization that was modeled on Hitler's Brown Shirts. Of course, the United States also played host to the German-American Bund, which claimed in 1939 to have more than 22,000 members.

Much better organized and more widespread than these fascist groups, however, were the left-wing associations that were encouraged by the economic hard times. These associations—many of which were infiltrated and controlled by the American Communist Party—included such pacifistic, Popular Front agencies as the Student League for Industrial Democracy, the American Student Union, the National Student League, and the American Youth Congress (the latter an amalgamation of some 4,000 local and national youth groups). The largest of the Popular Front organizations, the American League for Peace and Democracy, including its affiliates, may have had up to seven million members at the height of its influence. Also on the far left of the political spectrum were the John Reed Clubs, formed between 1932 and 1935 by disaffected intellectuals who desired a forum for the discussion of "proletarian" issues by the country's writers and artists. Within the acting profession, left-wingers associated themselves with the Theater Collective, the Theater Union, and the Group Theater, to produce propaganda plays across the United States. Ironically, so deeply rooted was the tradition of voluntary associations in America that fascist and communist propaganda and plots had to find a forum in what is fundamentally a vehicle for free government.[5]

After the outbreak of war in Europe in 1939, many more voluntary associations came together to promote or to resist a more active American role on the international scene. Leading the isolationist cause was the America First Committee, the members of which included an odd assortment of pacifists, idealists, Communists, socialists, Anglophobes, pro-Nazis, and old Midwestern Progressives. On the other side of the issue were ranged associations like the Non-Partisan Committee for Peace through Revision of the Neutrality Laws, which was called into being under the leadership of William Allen White after the Nazi destruction of Czechoslovakia. Reorganized in the spring of 1940 as the Committee to Defend America by Aiding the Allies, this association had more than 750 local chapters by the end of the year, and its 10,000 active workers and nearly one million members assumed a major leadership role in the nationwide effort to combat isolationist sentiment. Even at their most aggressive, however, the Committee's pronouncements did not go far enough for some of its members, who broke away in early 1941 to organize the Fight for Freedom Committee and agitate for outright American entry into the war.

As might be expected, once the country was plunged into the war, there was a great surge in the number of volunteer organizations devoted to home defense, civilian protection, and civilian war services. The National Legion of the Mothers of America immediately organized a Molly Pitcher Brigade to pick off descending parachutists. In Tillamook, Oregon, and Lexington, Massachusetts, middle-aged men formed themselves into self-proclaimed guerrilla bands, to harass whatever Japanese or German forces might someday land on America's shores. All over the country, home guard units, loosely patterned on the much-renowned Home Guard of Britain, sprang into existence. In Carson City, the local Home Guard consisted of just twenty-five volunteers; in Miami, however, the McAllister Volunteers enrolled 400 persons; and in Chapel Hill,

North Carolina, Mrs. Virginia Nowell, formerly of the Chapel Hill PTA, succeeded in organizing a 1,000-member, all-female unit known as the Green Guards.

With a large percentage of the nation's able-bodied men engaged in military service, women formed the backbone of many other wartime associations. In scores of small towns, women took over the entire responsibility for the volunteer fire brigades. Women also assumed leadership roles in the thousands of local groups that devoted themselves to sponsoring "drives" to collect rubber, paper, scrap metal, and whatever other surplus materials might be useful to the war effort. Meanwhile, the 260,000 members of the American Women's Volunteer Service were actively engaged in such tasks as driving trucks, making maps, rolling bandages, staffing information centers, and providing instruction on the procedures to be followed in the event of air raids.

Inspired by wartime patriotism, thousands of other local and national volunteer groups did what they could to further the Allied cause. The Junior League and the High School Victory Corps provided young people to harvest victory gardens. The Minute Men sold war bonds on street corners. More than 300 relief organizations collected money and other items for war relief in Europe and Asia (by the end of 1941, the largest of these associations, Bundles for Britain, had a half-million members and over a thousand local chapters). Providing civil defense services, meanwhile, were some 11,000 Local Defense Councils, enrolling ten million citizens as air raid wardens, couriers, auxiliary police, and medical workers. Also contributing to local defense were the 600,000 members of the Ground Observer Corps, who manned aircraft spotter posts and reported suspicious aircraft to the appropriate military centers.

FOOTNOTES

[1] Edward O. Guerrant, *Herbert Hoover, Franklin D. Roosevelt, Comparisons and Contrasts,* pp. 51-53. On June 16, 1933, Roosevelt said, "... if all employers in each trade now band themselves faithfully in these modern guilds—without exception—and agree to act together and at once, none will be hurt ... We are relaxing some of the safeguards of the anti-trust laws." See also Arthur M. Schlesinger, Jr. *The Coming of the New Deal,* pp. 87-102

[2] *Ibid.,* pp. 37-38 and 77-78

[3] Arthur M. Schlesinger, Jr., *The Politics of Upheaval,* pp. 593-594

[4] *Ibid.,* pp. 15-124

[5] Irving Howe and Lewis Coser, *The American Communist Party,* pp. 352-355

Chapter Twelve The Age of the Political Action Committee

As we have seen, voluntary associations in America come in all sizes, exist to foster a myriad of purposes, and seek to influence the political process directly through involvement in election campaigns, and indirectly through education programs for their members and the public. The present form, however, of the modern day Political Action Committee goes back to the Non-Partisan League of the Great Depression, and its successor organization, the Council of Industrial Organizations Political Action Committee, founded in 1943 largely in response to the growing power of the anti-labor bloc in Congress. Thus, the modern day Political Action Committee grew out of the struggle of American labor to influence election outcomes.

Determined to secure the re-election of President Roosevelt in 1944, the CIO PAC set about the task by dispatching thousands of PAC members into working-class neighborhoods in the months before the election, to register previously apathetic voters and to encourage them to cast their ballots. "Let's quit blaming the politicians and face the responsibility of full citizenship," said one PAC brochure. "Let's become politicians ourselves."[1] Though it was frequently damned by Dewey and the Republicans, the CIO PAC may have been responsible for as many as six million Democratic votes in 1944—a particularly potent performance in light of the fact that the margin of Roosevelt's plurality was only about three million votes.

The antecedents of the business political action committee date from the turn of the century. In 1904, public opinion was excited over allegations that the corporations of America had poured millions of dollars into Republican coffers to elect Teddy Roosevelt. Outcries were heard from no lesser personages than Charles Evans Hughes (later Chief Justice), William Jennings Bryan, Charles William Eliot, and Samuel Gompers. These men and other formed the National Publicity Law Association (NPLA), and urged Congress to enact strict regulation of corporate spending in federal campaigns. In 1907, Congress passed the first substantial legislation restricting corporate contributions. The Tillman Act, designed to curb corporate influence in elective politics, ironically generated the modern day Business Political Action Committee. It was this particular piece of government intervention into the relations of business and politics that forced business to look for new vehicles of influence.

The Tillman Act initially restricted only corporate gifts of money to federal elective offices or to committees supporting candidates. This was later modified to forbid corporate contributions of "anything of value" when the provisions of this act were incorporated in the Federal Corrupt Practices Act of 1925. The FCPA, although made law during a period of relative goodwill between government and business, was in part a reaction to Tea Pot Dome. The effort to restrict the involvement of business and industry in politics has been genuinely bi-partisan, occurring under Republican as well as Democratic administrations.

Filling the vacuum left by the 1907 and 1925 laws was the emergence of trade associations, such as the Edison Electric Institute, the American Bankers Association, the National Association of Manufacturers, and the United States Chamber of Commerce (which was formed as the result of a White House sponsored conference held in 1912). These and other like associations sought to influence legislative outcomes, not by current electoral methods, but by traditional lobbying techniques.

In 1943, moved by the inordinate amount of campaign contributions made by labor unions in the 1936 and 1940 elections—contributions that were taken from mandatory union dues—the Smith-Connally Act became law. This act imposed the same election restrictions on labor unions that had up until this time solely been the burden of business. Unions, their fund raising and spending capabilities impaired, turned their energies into political education and the utilization of their members for get-out-the-vote and registration drives, phone banks, polling operations, and candidate research. All of these efforts were funded directly out of union dues and from contributions by affiliates to the AF of L and to the CIO. Business efforts during this period were meager by comparison, although some effort was put into the cultivation and organization of candidates with a pro-business point of view.

Business had much to do if it was going to catch up with the experience of labor. But nothing happened until 1961, when the medical profession launched its own political action movement. The American Medical Political Action Committee (AMPAC) was formed with the American Medical Association's official blessing as a voluntary, non-profit, unincorporated organization whose purpose, according to Joe D. Miller, who guided the birth and important first years of AMPAC as its Executive Director until 1968, was to "help its members participate effectively in public affairs; further their knowledge; and develop the means for concerted political action." Autonomous medical political action committees soon began operating in each of the fifty states as well as the District of Columbia, with members contributing to the state PAC and AMPAC. These contributions were used to support political candidates, but the medical PAC's stressed involvement in campaigns and political parties as well.

The success of the medical profession's political action movement, and the encouragement which medical leaders gave to business, industry, and other professions, soon spawned the creation of the Business and Industry Political Action Committee, formed by the National Association of Manufacturers in 1963. According to Kenton R. Cravens, Chairman of the Board for Eagle Rubber Company and Director of American Zinc Company, and BIPAC's first Chairman, "BIPAC will be a new force in politics . . . and will strive to advance the principles of individual freedom, and those of free enterprise." [2] Thus began what has been called by many "the PAC revolution."

Using AMPAC & BIPAC as models, many associations sprouted PACs—National Association of Realtors (Realtors PAC), National Automobile Dealers Association (Automobile and Truck Dealers Election Action Committee), and American Dental Association (American Dental PAC), to name a few.

These and other types of PAC's continued to proliferate across the country—gaining power and influence until 1971, when Congress passed the Federal Election Campaign Act. The FECA of 1971, and its subsequent revisions in 1974, 1976, and 1980, regulated both individual and PAC contributions in the electoral marketplace—although it impeded the former more significantly than the latter—by limiting individual contributions to federal candidates to $1,000 and requiring candidates to establish one committee that would handle all their contributions and expenditures. The effort of the 1971 Act was immediate—Americans, their individual freedom impaired, turned to voluntary associations, as they have done traditionally, to express their political minds. It was beginning in 1971, with the passage of the FECA, that the recent explosion in the number of business PAC's began. Between 1971 and 1975 the number of business PAC's in the United States grew from a handful to 140. Contributions from these groups to federal candidates reached the $2 million level in 1974.

In 1975, the newly formed Federal Election Commission released an opinion allowing Sun Oil Company to found a political action committee using corporate monies to administer and solicit funds for the SunPAC. The ruling also permitted Sun Oil to use company funds to establish a separate voluntary payroll deduction plan for its employees. Further, it was decided, Sun Oil could maintain multiple PACs as long as the contributions for these PACs came solely from voluntary contributions.[3]

With the Sun Oil decision, the dam was broken, and corporations began organizing speedily the nationwide development of PACs. By 1978, there were 1,938 political action committees registered with the Federal Election Commission and collecting and spending funds for 1978 federal candidates alone. Of the 1,938 PACs, 821 corporate PACs gave $9.8 million to federal candidates; 543 trade, membership/health PACs gave $11.5 million to federal candidates; 281 labor PACs gave $10.3 million to federal candidates; and 293 other political action committees gave $3.5 million to federal candidates. A total of $35.1 million was contributed by political action committees to federal candidates. Federal candidates spent a total of $192 million in 1978. PAC contributions represented 17% of that total.

Since 1978, Congress has been under significant pressure from the "left" to further restrict the actions of political action committees. Crying "tyranny of the special interests," these groups point to the geometric growth of business PAC expenditures and advocate public financing of federal elections.

Although the tradition of voluntary associations remains strong in contemporary America, it has expressed itself most dramatically in the development of the Political Action Committee. Earlier it was pointed out that the antecedent to the modern day business political action committee dates from 1907 legislation restricting the contribution of corporate money to candidates for federal office. Going back to the Sons of Liberty, many of our most prominent voluntary associations were generated as a result of government interference in the lives of Americans. The Political Action Committee, however, more than most, has been the particular object of government scrutiny, legislation, and regulation. Indeed, it is particularly as a result of the 1971 Federal Elections Campaign Act and the Sun Oil decision, that the nation has witnessed a boom in Political Action Committees, and that discussion about them has become so intense. For those who oppose the political action committee and seek some form of governmental intervention for alleged wrongs, it has never been more true to say: they have no one to blame but government.

Perhaps the Political Action Committee demonstrates better than most examples of voluntary associations the flexibility, creativity, and general utility of this institute with regard to the conditions of a free society. Americans have almost always addressed difficult times through the vehicle of voluntary association. The hardest times, however, have been their engagements with government over interests and principles they hold dear. In the case of the Political Action Committee it was not only generated by government intervention, but has had continually to respond, since creation, to the will of government. Still political action committees persist, vital, useful, and a salutary influence on the political system. Perhaps this more than any other example testifies to how deeply rooted the tradition of voluntary association is in the marrow of American life.

FOOTNOTES

[1] James Foster, *The Union Politic: The CIO Political Action Committee,* pp. 24-26
[2] George D. Webster, *Business and Professional Political Action Committees,* p. 32
[3] Edwin Epstein, *Corporations, Contributions, and Political Campaigns: Federal Regulation in Perspective,* p. 16

Section IV
The Political Action Committee in Law and Public Policy

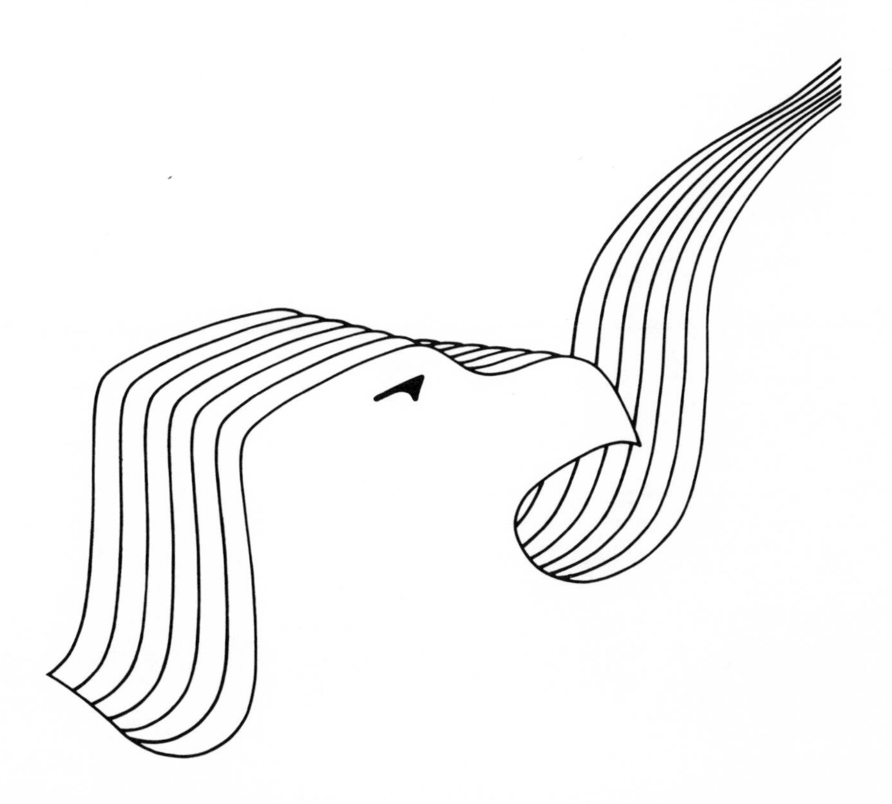

Chapter Thirteen
The Law

In the last chapter we saw that political action committees evolved as a result of government intervention in the economy. In this chapter we discuss political committees in light of the laws regulating them and the attitudes toward them of public policy makers.

Although the activities of interest groups, including political action committees, are protected by the First Amendment as a form of political speech, tax and campaign finance laws restrict how money may be collected, handled, and expended. The following listings show the major statutes, court decisions, and other government actions that have shaped the growth of today's political action committee.

1907-Tillman Act This act prohibited corporations from contributing money to campaigns in federal elections. Subsequent amendments by Congress were made to embody all contributions and expenditures, not only money, and to include primary elections and nominating conventions. The act, with its amendments, remained virtually unchanged for 65 years.

1925-Corrupt Practices Act This statute set limits on the amount that any particular political committee could receive or spend, and also limited individual contributions of money or in-kind services to the candidate in federal elections. It required that all campaign receipts and expenditures be reported in detail to the Clerk of the House, and the Secretary of the Senate. It did not, however, limit overall spending in Senate and House campaigns.

1940-Hatch Act The Hatch Act imposed spending limits on presidential campaigns as follows: no amount in excess of $3 million could be spent by the candidate or committee; all receipts and expenditures had to be filed with the Clerk of the House; and no more than $5,000 could be given to a candidate or a committee operating in two or more states.

1943-Smith-Connally Act This act applied to labor unions throughout the war. It was Congress' response to large labor contributions during the previous two national elections. It put the same restrictions on unions that corporations had dealt with for 36 years.

1947-Taft-Hartley Act In essence, Taft-Hartley was the peace-time extension of the 1943 War Disputes (Smith-Connally) Act. It prohibited union contributions and expenditures in federal elections, primary and general, and in nominating conventions.

1971-Federal Election Campaign Act (FECA) The FECA revolutionized PAC's by legislatively legitimizing the political committee and prescribing its form and method of operation. It allowed corporations, labor unions, and other associations to:

1) Communicate on any subject (including partisan politics) to stockholders and members, respectively, and their families.
2) Conduct non-partisan registration and get-out-the-vote campaigns directed at these same constituencies.
3) Establish and administer a "Separate segregated fund" to be utilized for political purposes (i.e., to set up a political action committee).

1972-Pipefitters Local #562 v. United States This was the first court case judged on the grounds of the FECA. The union was indicted with several of its officials for maintaining a political fund by means of mandatory contributions from its members. Concurrently, a separate "voluntary" fund was maintained by funds strictly segregated from union dues and assessments. However, this was controlled by union officials who systematically collected members' contributions. The union and a few of its officials were convicted of violating federal law on the grounds that the fund was not voluntary, but rather compulsory and union-financed.

1974-FECA Amendments In 1974 an amendment was added to the FECA which created the Federal Election Commission (FEC) whose purpose was to administer federal election laws. Unquestionably, for business, labor, and other association PAC's, the most important aspect of this amendment was the clarification of the section relating to government contractors. It held that the restrictions on campaign contributions and expenditures by government contractors did not prohibit labor unions or corporations from establishing and maintaining political action committees.

1974-Sun Oil Within three months of the creation of the FEC the Sun Oil Company requested it to rule on a potential PAC which they were in the process of forming. This PAC included a political contributions program for employees (SUN-EPA). Sun proposed using general corporate funds to establish, administer, and solicit voluntary contributions to a PAC (SUN-PAC). In addition Sun Oil wished to create the separate payroll deduction plan. The FEC ruled that:

1) General corporate funds could be used by Sun Oil to establish, administer, and solicit contributions to both SUN-PAC and SUN-EPA.
2) Contributions to SUN-PAC could be solicited from both stockholders and employees. (This was important in that the FEC made clear that corporations could use general treasury funds to solicit contributions not only from stockholders and their families, but also their employees).
3) Multiple PAC's with separate contribution and expenditure limits were permissible as long as the monies came only from voluntary contributions.

This ruling upset the fragile political balance that Congress had so carefully sought to establish between corporations and unions (e.g., Sun Oil had approximately 127,000 shareholders and 28,000 employees, of which a small percentage were unionized. Thus, the corporation could solicit over 155,000 individuals—many more than the union).

1976-Buckley v. Valeo In 1976, in this case, the Supreme Court determined the constitutionality of major provisions of the 1971 FECA as amended in 1974. It ruled that the Federal Election Commission was unconstitutional as a consequence of the manner in which the FEC commissioners were appointed. This Supreme Court ruling indicated that the 1974 act had not limited the number of PAC's which could be established by various branches of corporations and unions (e.g. subsidiaries or divisions; local and regional units of national labor unions). The court ruled that each such PAC had a separate $5,000 contribution limit, provided that it acted "independently of control or direction by the parent corporation or the national or regional union." Finally, the court, in essence, authorized "independent" expenditures (those services done without the knowledge or request of the candidate or his representatives).

1976-FECA Amendments In 1976 an amendment to the FECA was brought into being which gave a significant advantage to unions. Permission was granted to a union to utilize payroll deduction plans (check-offs) among its members, as long as the company PAC used the same method among its stockholders, executives, and administrative personnel. It made clear that while a corporation could set up an infinite number of PAC's, a single $5,000 per candidate, per election contribution limit would be placed upon all such committees. Finally, it restricted the ability of PAC's to pool funds for large contributions to a single candidate by restricting transfers in excess of $5,000 to affiliated PAC's.

If the efforts of government to restrict corporate involvement in the political process characterize the greater part of twentieth century American history, the decade of the seventies brought a whole new dimension to the relationship of business and politics. In 1971 Congress passed the most comprehensive campaign financing reform bill ever. The Federal Election Act of 1971 legitimized the business political action committee and, by the end of the decade, labor found itself in sharp competition with business in the area of dispensing campaign contributions. Specifically, the major provisions of the 1971 act were as follows: 1) Corporations are now permitted, through the mechanism of the PAC, to send political communications to the stockholders of the company and their families; 2) Corporations are permitted to organize and conduct, using company money, registration and get-out-the-vote campaigns aimed at stockholders and their families; and 3) Corporations are reaffirmed in their right to establish and administer a "separate and segregated fund" to be utilized for political purposes (the right to form a PAC).

Prior to the passage of the FECA, the United States Supreme Court was considering the case of Pipefitters Local #562 v. United States 407 U.S. 385 (1972). The Court waited decision on this case until after the passage of the FECA, at which time it convicted the union of maintaining a political fund, by means of mandatory union dues, and of creating a separate "voluntary fund" which, although technically separate from all union dues, was controlled by union officials who systematically influenced members into donating. That a federal court was needed to intervene in and consider a case of this nature—involving events likely to recur—suggested to Congress that an enforcement and monitoring mechanism was needed. In 1974, therefore, Congress passed a set of amendments to the 1971 FECA. The most advertised part of these amendments was the section creating the Federal Election Commission (FEC); but what was most important to business and labor was the section relating to government contractors. It held that the restrictions on campaign contributions by government contractors—a restriction that made many corporations uneasy about forming a political committee—applied neither to labor unions nor political committees in general.

A further critical development occurred shortly afterwards. In a redefinition of the 1974 amendments, the FEC ruled that Sun Oil Company could solicit funds from *both* its stockholders *and* its employees. It also held that both labor unions and corporations could maintain multiple affiliate political associations, so long as the monies came from separate voluntary contributions.[1] These rulings constitute the most important developments relating to the re-entry of corporate contributions into the political arena since the 1907 Tillman Act. As a result, between the 1974 Sun Oil ruling and the present, some hundreds of corporations formed political committees. By 1980, it is estimated, there will be 1000 federal business political action committees in the United States.

FOOTNOTES

[1] Edwin Epstein, *Corporations, Contributions, and Political Campaigns: Federal Regulation in Perspective*, pp. 16-17

Chapter Fourteen Public Policy Makers and the PAC

Not surprisingly, few policy makers, whether legislators or executives or bureaucrats, can be found to defend the PAC and its role in politics. Most elective officials dislike, even resent, the necessity of raising money to fund their campaigns; many prefer public financing as a trouble-free, assured alternative. Similarly, executives and bureaucrats know that their lives would be easier, group pressures in the policy arena less troubling and effective, if PAC's were shut out of the process.

At bottom, the hostile attitude of elective officials toward PAC's traces to their dislike of *competition*. As vigorous participants in the political system, PAC's represent a competitive force, one to which policy-makers must accommodate and with which they must reckon. Public financing, by contrast, would reduce the competitive pressures on officials, narrowing the constituencies to which they must respond. (Of course, the case for public financing is partly made from this perspective.)

The public interest in easing the lives of policy makers, however, is slight. Indeed, the case for the PAC rests in part on its capacity to bring new pressures to bear on the policy process, to interest more citizens in campaigns and issues, and to force officials better to frame and defend their policies. If the proponents of the PAC were wise—or as astute in public relations as its critics are—they would make their stand on this ground. Public financing is anti-competitive, a means of adding to the official monopoly of the policy process; the PAC can help build a more competitive political system.

Some of the hostility of public policy makers toward PAC's traces, also, to ideological bias. The accusation, now quite common, that PAC contributions are morally tantamount to "bribes" is made by opponents of business and the free market. What they really mean by the accusation, of course, is that if they had their way, they would run the system differently—that is, to their own advantage and against business interests. Their fear is that the growth of non-union political contributions, and the re-emergence of business dollars in politics, will give business attitudes greater weight and perhaps lead to more market solutions to policy problems. Such critics can not be satisfied by any procedural checks. It is not enough that business PAC's function in an open, publicly organized way, or that they meet the requirements of a most complicated body of statute law, court decisions, and FEC rulings; these critics want business PAC's outlawed from politics.

One common argument is that business has come to "dominate" politics through the use of PAC's. The evidence cited for this criticism is the increase in the number of committees organized by business in the last six years, and the volume of dollars contributed by those committees to candidates. But, as Michael J. Malbin has shown:

> *PAC's are but a small part of the campaign/finance story—though the part that gets all the publicity. They are indeed contributing more money to campaigns than they used to, and that trend is likely to continue. But the other half of the story—the unpublicized half—reveals a trend that is at least as important. PAC's may have given 50 percent more to Congressional candidates in 1978 than in 1976, but so did everyone else. PAC's therefore, were responsible for about the same percentage of all Congressional-campaign contributions in 1978 as in 1976. They were proportionately more important in 1976 than in 1974, but that fact simply reflected a change in the style of business giving because of the new law.*[1]

The difference, then, between 1976 and 1978, Malbin concludes, is that "campaigns became more expensive." [2] Much of this is due to inflation. Some of it is due to the fact that, after a long lull as a result of Watergate, Republicans were seriously challenging Democrats for House and Senate seats—and convinced contributors of this. Genuine competition tends to boost the cost of campaigns.

Business political committees are far from threatening the system as a monolithic interest group. In 1978, while union committees gave 95 percent of their contributions to Democrats, business oriented committees divided their contributions between Republicans (60%) and Democrats (40%). If Republicans are the "party of business," and Democrats "the party of the working man," the point seems to have escaped corporate, trade, and professional political action committees. Perhaps, some will suggest, PAC's own both political parties! But if this is the case, how does one prove that a House Member is "owned?" For example, in 1978, out of a total trade and professional association contribution of $10.7 million, AMPAC contributed $1,563,000, Realtors Political Action Committee $1,170,000, and Automobile and Truck Dealers Election Action Committee $970,000. If a Representative is "owned" does that involve a vote for the interests of medicine or for real estate or for cars and trucks? On many issues, including tax, these interest groups have widely divergent concerns and needs.

As to the charge that big business monopolizes the PAC market place, one must examine the facts to make an objective analysis. Of all the business related PAC's operating in the United States today, only 14.3% are affiliated with companies in the "Fortune 500." An even smaller percentage—10.6%—represent companies that rank 501-1300. In short, medium-sized and small business PAC's in America today outnumber big business PAC's by a better than 3-1 margin. It is also interesting to note that of the ten largest PAC contributors in the 1978 elections, none was a business PAC—indeed, the largest business PAC contribution in 1978 was $173,056, compared with the $964,465 given by the United Auto Workers PAC, and the $920,841 given by the AFL-CIO PAC. The statistics regarding average contributions paint a similar scene. While the average contribution by labor PAC's to incumbents was $607.33 in 1978, corporations averaged only $289.21; labor contributions to challengers and to open seats averaged $863.52 and $1,296.26 respectively, while corporations contributed an average of only $381.71 and $416.83 respectively. The force of these statistics is compelling. Contrary to popular myth—so popular, that it is believed within and outside the business community alike—business is far from monopolizing the financing of federal elections.

It is rarely noted, either by the critics or supporters of business PAC's, that one reason for their growth is that, since the FECA reforms of the early 1970's, individuals have lost the ability to make large contributions to campaigns. Business PAC's have helped fill the vacuum. Thus, the wealthiest PAC's are those with a broad constituency, large groupings of individuals who wish to give weight to their preferences for candidates and issues. For many years, the standard argument (never seriously challenged until the emergence of the business PAC) for the committee activity of unions in politics was that individual union members lacked the ability to contribute meaningful sums—only by joining with other union members of similar interests could they have influence. But today, the same argument applies to business PAC's—they provide a means whereby large numbers of individuals can have influence in the political process.

PAC's serve an even more useful purpose than the simple administration of individual contributions. They assemble constituencies for the broad issues of the day. Since the birth of representative democracy, men have argued the true purpose of an elected official. On the "delegate" side of the issue, it is argued that an elected official must represent—almost mathematically—the views of his constituents. The opposing view is that the representative should act the part of the "trustee," voting and advocating the issues he perceives to be in the best interest of his constituency or the nation. In Congress today, most members seem to subscribe more to the "delegate" conception of their duties. The political action committee, whether it represents labor, business, trade associations, or professional groups, acts as a counterbalance to the provinciality of a Congress based on single member districts. Political action committees assemble members across congressional district boundaries, around issues that transcend the interests of a particular city, county, or region. The questions of gun ownership, abortion, nationalized medicine, labor laws, foreign policy—issues much debated in Congress—do impact some congressional districts more than others, but ultimately affect the nation as a whole much more. Should the present trends in the legislation regarding PAC's continue, and the political action committee become a thing of the past, how will groups of citizens, great in number, but dispersed among many congressional districts, make their views heard in that national forum we call the United States Congress?

Above all, the heterogeneity of American business and professional groups suggests that PAC's, rather than endangering the political system, in fact enhance it. In the spirit of Madison, the more political committees that are generated, the greater the multiplicity of interests that will be promoted and, thus, the more individuals that will find a home in the political system.

These and other advantages of political committees can be mentioned without failing to recognize possible areas of concern. This is especially important for those who, seeking to maintain the vitality of PAC involvement in American politics, need a defensive as well as an offensive strategy. For example, the tendency of PAC's to contribute to incumbents only adds to the already powerful asset of incumbency at election time. Although PAC supporters denounce public financing of election campaigns, they inadvertently contribute to the same protection from electoral competition secretly wished for by public officials promoting public financing by favoring incumbents with their dollars. PAC members should recall that the history of political associations in America has more often than not been a history of support for the "underdog" or the "little guy" struggling against the impositions of government. Officials and members of political committees should be alert to the possibility that their resources are capable of strengthening the very elected officials who threaten their rights and interests.

In addition, political action committees too often look for short run political gains, rather than focusing on the long range development of candidates—a function for which they are ideally suited. Because of the nature of the American political system, candidate recruitment tends to be neglected (although much is said about it) by the two major political parties. Indeed, most candidates for public office select themselves with little outside support or encouragement from anyone other than immediate family and associates. Political committees could redress this fault line in our practical politics, looking for promising candidates who, seeking office for the first time, need seed money and "in-kind" materials to launch a realistic campaign. PAC's, for instance, could provide research materials or sponsor "how to" training sessions for potential candidates, supplying them with valuable instruction in the character of a district or the art of political campaigning. Political committees could also share the burden of relieving the debt of a promising but losing candidate—of a person who made a "good stab" at a first run for office, and, with the proper encouragement, might "make it" on the second try. Moreover, committees should be alert to bright and able legislators at the local and state levels of government, grooming them for higher office statewide and nationally. Furthermore, PAC's should not select candidates merely on the basis of whether they "go down the line" for a particular economic or social interest; rather, they should look to support candidates who are dedicated to the general principles of a free and competitive society. Many elected officials will vote for the interests of a particular industry or union on a specific bill, although their overall legislative record or political philosophy is one that favors the public over the private sector.

Although one of the heralded functions of political action committees is political education, little time and few resources are given to meaningful programs. Too often "quickie" communiques and newsletters about the immediate interests of a union, an industry, a trade, or a profession take the place of sound and substantial education about the general principles of American democracy underlying all private interests. Training in the art of politics, including how union, professional, and company members can get involved in the political process—from precinct organization through techniques for fund raising to the sophisticated use of data and polling results—have a long range "pay off" to the PAC membership that significantly complements the practice of "writing your Representative" when a hostile bill is pending before the legislature. If PAC's devote more of their resources to their long-range functions and purposes, political action committees will not only meet some of the specific charges of their critics, but, in addition, create a more substantial foundation for permanent institutional success.

It is part of the American faith that voluntary associations are the nursery of Democracy. We worry today about apathy and about the growth in the powers of government. The political committee speaks to both concerns. Its capacity to educate, to heighten interest in candidates and issues by raising money, and to stimulate individual involvement in campaigns—these are surely salutary activities, and needful in a time when millions of Americans fail even to perform the most basic responsibility of citizenship. As Tocqueville understood, the voluntary association stands, too, as a fundamental check on the powers of government. Those powers will increase if public financing replaces private contributions as the means of funding campaigns. We will preserve and promote the political committee if we do not wish to yield to government a monopoly of the most important of all the processes of a representative democracy—its elections.

FOOTNOTES

[1] Michael J. Malbin, *Parties, Interest Groups and Campaign Finance Laws*, p. 127
[2] *Ibid.*, p. 129

Chapter Fifteen
Epilogue

Although the interest group structure of American politics was anticipated by the authors of the *Federalist*, and to some extent was approached in the writings of early sociologists and economists, its formal study by political scientists did not begin until the middle of the twentieth century. Today there exists a flood of research and publications providing "hard" empirical data to confirm the special role of voluntary associations within the American experience.

One finding stands out above all others. Although Americans belong to business, professional, and charitable associations in approximately the same percentage as citizens of Great Britain, Germany, and Italy, two kinds of voluntary associations attract Americans in significantly larger numbers: political and religious associations.[1] Almost one fifth of all adult Americans belong to religious associations as compared to one-twentieth of the countries mentioned above. Similarly, roughly 11 percent of the adult population in America belong to a civic or political organization—three times the number who belong to such associations in Britain or Germany. Furthermore, when citizens from a variety of countries were asked what they would do to protest an unfair local law, 56 percent of the Americans said that they would organize letter writing campaigns among their neighbors, sign petitions, and take other actions to bring to bear the weight of the local community. By contrast, only 34 percent of the British and

13 percent of the Germans offered similar responses.[2] What Tocqueville observed in America in 1830 was not merely a passing phase of the nation's history, but rather continues to characterize the topography of its society and politics today.

Perhaps this activity testifies, as some believe, to a superior sense of civic duty on the part of American citizens.[3] Other reasons for the proliferation of voluntary associations can be studied in light of American history, culture, and political institutions. For instance, the fact that Americans today are inclined to think of political and other forms of association as an effective way of influencing government must be set down to a habit of the political culture. The lessons of one generation have been transmitted to another so that the formation of voluntary associations as the means to almost any end is now "second nature" to almost all Americans.

The political culture of Americans is reinforced by the nation's political institutions. For instance, there are at least three major farm organizations in the United States, and while there is only one American Medical Association and one American Medical Political Action Committee, there are also state medical societies, along with state medical political action committees affording doctors significant access to the political process.

The proliferation of voluntary organizations in the United States is directly related to the federal division of power among the national government, the states, and localities, and the separation of powers within each level of government. These divisions of jurisdiction and power provide opportunities for access to the political process by citizens in numbers and ways that are almost unknown in other countries. The multiplicity of divisions within the American structure of government offers some opportunity to almost everyone to influence their elected and appointed leaders, and is the fertile ground from which associations for nearly any cause spring into being. By contrast, in Great Britain there is only one organization for farmers, a single organization for veterans, one major business organization, and a single medical society. Since decisions affecting these groups are made nationally by an appropriate ministry, the tendency in Britain has been to consolidate members into one organization for purposes of effective relationships with the central governmental authority.[4]

Political institutions, of course, do not account entirely for the tradition of voluntary associations in America. The Soviet Union is a federal system, yet the ability of its citizens to influence the government or the party through private, voluntary action is severely limited by the absence of the principles and the practices of freedom.

The structure of American political parties also contributes to the abundance of interest groups. In Europe, political parties are strong and controlled from the top, and interest group activity is weak. In America, by comparison, political parties are weak and interest group activity is strong. The relative weakness of American political parties is in part the result of the separation between the executive and the legislative branches of government. In comparison with a candidate for the British parliament, who is appointed by his party to run in a given constituency, the candidate for Congress receives little help from his party, begins by cultivating his own grass roots organization, raises his own campaign funds, and once elected, can challenge the wishes of the party or of the leader of the party (even if he be the President) on issues of concern to his own constituents. Furthermore, because the total number of votes in the electoral college is divided along the lines of the federal principle, the "natural" home of American political parties is in the states and not in the headquarters of the Democratic or Republican National Committees in Washington.

As a result of the decentralized party system, parties in America tend to be less ideological than European parties and more concerned with coalition building. Andrew Jackson was, perhaps, the first American to fully grasp the potential for building relationships between interest groups and party government. He built his party on the basis of an interest group coalition—a legacy which continues to characterize American politics.

The roles of interest groups in the political arena are well known. They provide special services to the electorate and to government officials that would otherwise be unavailable short of government itself. They supply technical information to the government—as, for example, before Congressional committees—that would otherwise require hours of staff time and government salaries to obtain. They educate the public in newspaper ads and on radio and television regarding their particular interests and their relationship to the overall health of the economy and the nation. And they provide votes and money for candidates. Although this is an area of great controversy today, there continue to be many benefits from interest group financing of campaigns. The ability of an office seeker to raise money from a coalition of private interests demonstrates his viability as a candidate. It also suggests his ability to be a representative—to reflect and work with a number of viewpoints necessary for election.

Interest groups also soften the risk of political involvement for ordinary citizens. To act in association with others is to gain strength and courage for one's interest and principles, allowing the average American to "speak up" where otherwise timidity might prevail. Indeed, interest groups also speak for the unaffiliated American, who vicariously enjoys the advantage and strength of an organized group pressing his concerns. After all, those who compose the true "silent majority" find little support in government, which often appears distant, impersonal, and preoccupied with matters that little affect their daily lives and concerns. Interest groups provide this segment of society with representation that they would not otherwise enjoy.

Finally, interest groups watch and monitor government, keeping it sensitive to the will of a substantial number of constituents, organizing voters to oppose measures harmful to perceived interests, checking the records of representatives, thus keeping them faithful to their districts and generally honest. In extreme circumstances, interest groups, such as civil rights organizations, antiwar protesters, and environmental organizations, can organize picketing and other forms of direct action to make their point to government officials "who won't listen." This form of interest group activity dates to the American Revolution—which might not have occurred without an already established tradition of private, voluntary group activity.

The role and function of interest group politics is as old as the American republic. Although only recently made a subject of scholarship, great strides have been taken in understanding the importance of interest groups to the success of American democracy. Ironically, just at the moment when our understanding is maturing, an attitude has developed that the involvement of interest groups in the political process is somehow ignoble and detrimental to the health of the democracy. This trend does not necessarily deny the role of interest groups in the political system, but rather singles out certain interests as "special," that is, as peculiarly harmful, because of their wealth and influence.

The colloquial definition of the term "special interest" is of quite recent origin. It is an ideologically charged term. For instance, Environmental Action, Inc., actively involves itself in elections (although not with campaign contributions). In 1970 it made public a list of thirty-one members of the House that it labeled the "Dirty Dozen." As of 1978, only seven of the original thirty-one members still held their seats in Congress. Yet, Environmental Action, Inc. is never spoken of as a "special interest;" indeed, to many of its ideological supporters, it is thought to be beyond interest, since it stands for a clean environment. Its record of achievement would make many supposedly more powerful groups, such as the American Medical Political Action Committee and the Business and Industry Political Action Committee, envious. Yet, that they are labeled "special interests," and Environmental Action, Inc. escapes that designation, can be due only to ideological bias. Environmental Action, Inc., along with AMPAC and BIPAC are, from the standpoint of morality, law, and political tradition, equally interest groups. Adequate public education only—a function well suited to political action committees—will lay the myth of "special" interest to rest.

FOOTNOTES

[1] James Q. Wilson, *American Government*, p. 210

[2] *Ibid.*

[3] *Ibid.*

[4] Wilson, pp. 206-207